FRENCH

FROM THE MARKET

FRENCH

FROM THE MARKET

HILLARY DAVIS

Gibbs Smith

First Edition
28 27 26 25 24   5 4 3 2 1

Published by
Gibbs Smith
P.O. Box 667
Layton, Utah 84041

1.800.835.4993 orders
www.gibbs-smith.com

Designer: Sheryl Dickert
Art director: Ryan Thomann
Editor: Michelle Branson
Production designer: Virginia Snow

Printed and bound in China
Gibbs Smith books are printed on either recycled, 100 percent post-consumer waste, FSC-certified papers or on paper produced from sustainable PEFC-certified forest/controlled wood source. Learn more at www.pefc.org.

Library of Congress Control Number: 2023942102
ISBN: 978-1-4236-6488-8

CONTENTS

INTRODUCTION

The collection of recipes in this cookbook is rooted in the variety of dishes I learned to cook while living in France, from my very first days as a newlywed in Paris to later in life from my village neighbors in the South of France, and from many dining experiences in different regions of the country. They reflect my love for authentic, traditional French cuisine, with my personal touches.

When I first moved to Paris, our apartment on the rue Saint-Jean-Baptiste de la Salle had a tiny kitchen in which you could barely turn around—and no dishwasher. Our landlord was a lady who decided that, at age twenty-one, I should know how to make at least basic French dishes. She showed me how to make ratatouille from the packages in the grocery store that come with the traditional vegetables and herbs arranged inside. She also introduced me to the best local butcher, just around the corner, where I bought all my meats. Everything I made with those meats was a revelation, flavorful and pleasing. Until, one day, I happened to look up as I walked in the door and saw a horse's head. It took me a couple of months to venture into a butcher shop again. But those experiences settled into my understanding and accepting of a new culture, through its food.

I also lived on the boulevard Saint-Germain in Paris and spent most of my days there stopping at restaurants and hotels to read their menus, visiting open-air markets, dining in bistros, cafés, and Michelin-

star restaurants, and absorbing at a fast rate all that was on offer. I made new friends, one of whom gave rather elegant dinner parties. At one dinner before New Year's Eve, following the main course, she presented each guest with their own small wheel of very ripe Vacherin cheese and a silver spoon. Proust had his madeleines; I have the unforgettable memory of my first taste of that runny, luscious Vacherin. And, yes, most of us ate the whole thing smeared on slices of baguette.

Later, I was lucky to live in the South of France in a village called Bar-sur-Loup, high in the hills above the Riviera. My neighbor, who I lovingly called "madame," would invite me to cook alongside her, and through her I met her friends and their friends, who were all delightfully willing to teach me their tips and tricks and techniques. Others would call and invite me to accompany them to open-air markets so I could learn where to go and how to glean which was the best stall to find a perfect fragrant Cavaillon melon or the freshest wild herbs and mushrooms.

From the very beginning, my life in France was centered on food and the cycle of the seasons. This is the French way of life, and it makes me happy. Every morning, I would lie in bed thinking about what might be available, dream of what I could make with it, and grow excited to head out to the markets. A series of stops might include a butcher in Valbonne, or a fish vendor, or a fabulous cheese shop in Cannes, the mill in the next village to mine for olive oil, the end of a driveway down the road for goat cheese or eggs, or the open-air markets in Antibes or Nice for everything.

I shopped every day. That is my cooking style: fresh every day with a minimum of processing. Shopping, cooking, and dining at home are central to life in France.

I would cook from my garden as well, with its vegetables, fig and orange trees, and with the roadside herbs I would forage on my walks up the hill to the village for our daily baguettes.

We liked to think our olive oil came from our trees but, in truth, the process is that you gather your olives and drive them down to the olive mill in the village of Opio, where they toss them in with their olives to press and sell. In return for delivering our bundles to them we would leave with just-pressed oil.

My joy and feeling blessed to have lived in Bar-sur-Loup is boundless because that time fit my personality and interests perfectly, so much so that I want to share that joy with others through writing cookbooks. My first, *Cuisine Niçoise*, was an anthem to the unsung cuisine found near Nice, which is intriguing because

of its close proximity to Italy. Those local dishes are seldomly found elsewhere. This marriage of French and Italian cooking, using the products of that particular terroir, produces recipes like *tourte de blettes, la trouchia*, or *tout-nus,* an inexpensive healthy way of cooking that emphasizes fish and vegetables.

I wrote three more French cookbooks: *French Comfort Food*, which celebrated at-home cozy everyday cooking from all regions of France; *Le French Oven*, an ode to what I believe to be the best "Dutch ovens" in the world—those made in France! Then I wrote *French Desserts,* because what could be better than sharing recipes for France's deliriously delicious desserts?

This, *French from the Market*, will be my fifth French cookbook.

With all this said, I'd like to talk to you about the mystique of French cooking. Somewhere along the way, we became convinced that it is hard to do. Make a soufflé? Let me put your fears to rest. A soufflé is as easy to make as an omelet. You just need the right baking dish, confidence, and a recipe. Quenelles? So many tutorials and cookbooks wax lyrical about all the

things you must do right to produce quenelles. Yet, quenelles are very forgiving. They are dumplings. Just toss ingredients into a food processor and scoop that mixture into a bowl and form the quenelles. Italian gnocchi and tortellini are harder to make and more time-consuming than making quenelles.

I have included a recipe for quenelles on page 108. Why? Because I love them. And I want to show you how easy they are to make. That is also why I have included a recipe for *tarte Tatin* on page 205. It is so easy and quick, yet has the same spectacular flavor of a more formal French recipe. You don't always have to follow the techniques or rules of purists or students of *haute* French cuisine, but rather have a free hand to do what a French person in the countryside might do, which is celebrate produce and the quality of ingredients above technique or strict rules.

So, where did the fear and mystique around French cooking come from? Especially since French home cooking is provincial, farm and backyard-driven, and frugal.

It, perhaps, came from the celebration of haute cuisine. I am all for haute cuisine, or designer cuisine, and revel in dining in those very special restaurants. But they produce very special food, food of the gods, the kind of food that would be almost impossible for the everyday cook to reproduce easily at home. The French dine on haute cuisine on dress-up occasions; they cook provincial cuisine at home, every day.

Provincial cooking couldn't be simpler. Here is an example. Ideally, if you were creating the perfect meal, you would make your own chicken or beef stock from scratch. And the French do. But in today's fast-moving world, most use a store-bought chicken or beef cube for everyday meals. What could be simpler?

Another example: recipes asking you to have cheesecloth at hand so you can put together a bouquet garni, tie it with twine, and use it to flavor broths.

My neighbor just threw bay leaves, whole cloves, peppercorns, thyme, parsley, and this or that from the garden into the stockpot, then strained it out later. *Voilà.* Easy. No stress or rules. Still delicious.

I believe that the current cooking culture for the widespread population of France is driven by all the cooking magazines you find on newsstands, and equally by hand-me-down recipes and farmers' markets where the growers eagerly offer you their recipes to prepare their produce.

So, I encourage you to dive into French cuisine with the knowledge that it is not hard, it is delicious, it is economical, and it will provide you and your loved ones with infinitely delicious heartwarming memories. From a country where home cooking is an art, and using the freshest, finest ingredients is the rule of the land, not much can go wrong.

MISE EN PLACE

For much of my life I cooked at the last minute, preparing ingredients as I followed a recipe's instructions. But now that I work out of my home and juggle different projects during the day, I have learned the joy of *mise en place*—preparing and organizing all ingredients and equipment for a dish before starting to cook.

My way of doing this involves a big tray that I keep on my kitchen counter next to the stove and another tray that sits in my refrigerator for ingredients that need to be kept cool.

During the day, when I have a few free minutes here and there, I prepare ingredients for that night's supper and put them in order of use in small or medium bowls on my tray, using plastic wrap over the bowls to keep ingredients clean and intact. I might do one or two in the morning and three or four in the afternoon, so the day flies by, and near suppertime when I am tired, most of the work has already been done and I can relax and just enjoy cooking.

Practice mise en place, like they do in professional kitchens, to save time as you cook and to know whether you are missing something before it is too late. There are five agreed-upon steps for mise en place, and if you follow them, your cooking experience will be much happier:

1. Read the entire recipe and understand it before starting to work.
2. Gather all the ingredients and utensils asked for in the recipe.
3. Prepare and measure all the ingredients.
4. Place the ingredients in individual bowls, dishes, or containers.
5. Place the ingredients and utensils around the area where you will be cooking.

ABOUT THE RECIPES

IN THIS BOOK

O vens vary. I found that out the hard way years ago when I had to produce a soufflé for a photo session and it just wouldn't cooperate. Frustrated, I went out in search of an oven thermometer, came back, and discovered the oven was off by 40 degrees! So, use my timings and temperatures for the recipes in this cookbook that work in my oven, but know your oven and always monitor how your food is progressing before it is supposed to be finished.

My house salts are Maldon sea salt flakes, Maldon smoked sea salt flakes, the lovely herbal salt made by the French company A. Vogel, Le Saunier de Camargue fleur de sel, and Le Paludier de Guérande fleur de sel. I am a bit of a salt lover.

I am also a bit of a mustard lover. Amora mustard from Dijon and Moutarde de Meaux Pommery, in the stone jar, are my house mustards. Around the holidays or special occasions, I purchase Moutarde Royale au Cognac from Pommery. It's fabulous with ham.

The butter I use in recipes is typically unsalted so I can determine how much salt I want to taste in a dish. However, when I serve salt on the table or on a cheese board, I serve both unsalted butter and the French butters that have crunchy sea salt flakes in them.

I always use extra-virgin olive oil when I cook. And most of my recipes are written for four people unless otherwise noted.

Nos desserts Maison

- Mousse au chocolat
- Panna Cotta Fruits Rouge
- Crème brulée
- Baba au Rhum
- Délice aux marrons
- Ile Flottante
- Crème caramel
- Clafoutis aux poires

STARTERS

You can think of the recipes in this chapter as hors d'oeuvres, if you serve them to be shared or as small plates, for example, the Alpine Parsnip Hummus with Hazelnuts (page 25) or Gorgeous Pink Radish Rillettes (page 26). Or, serve them as starting dishes before the main course to raise the curtain and begin to excite the taste buds in anticipation of what is to follow.

Alpine Parsnip Hummus with Hazelnuts

ChaCha restaurant in Megève, in the French Alps, makes a "mountain hummus" with root vegetables and juniper berries, which I found fascinating. So, I came home inspired to recreate a root vegetable hummus. I've also seen restaurants in the mountains there make hummus with beets or pumpkin, seasonal vegetables they can get during winter ski season. I settled on making one with parsnips, and have grown to love it more than chickpea hummus. Serve the hummus with crackers or breadsticks.

1 tablespoon sea salt

2 pounds parsnips, trimmed, peeled, and cut into ½-inch pieces

4 garlic cloves, sliced

Juice of 1 ½ medium organic lemons, plus more as needed

2 teaspoons sea salt flakes, plus more as needed

½ cup tahini

2 tablespoons water

6 tablespoons extra-virgin olive oil, divided, plus 2 tablespoons (optional)

2 teaspoons honey

3 tablespoons hazelnuts

Fill a large pot, big enough to hold all the parsnips, with water and bring to a boil over high heat. Add the sea salt, toss in the parsnips, and let the water return to a boil. Gently boil the parsnips for 18 to 20 minutes until very soft. Drain and transfer to the bowl of a food processor.

Add the garlic, lemon juice, sea salt flakes, and tahini and process to combine. With the machine running, slowly pour in the water, then slowly pour in 4 tablespoons of oil in a stream and process until very smooth. Taste and add more sea salt flakes or lemon juice, as needed.

If you want the hummus fluffier, add the optional 2 tablespoons of oil and process. Transfer to a bowl and smooth the top.

In a small bowl, whisk the remaining 2 tablespoons of oil and honey to blend, then drizzle in a circle over the hummus.

Put the hazelnuts into a zip-top plastic bag and pound with a rolling pin, or smash in a mortar and pestle, until well crushed. Sprinkle the crushed hazelnuts over the circle of oil and serve.

Gorgeous Pink Radish Rillettes

SERVES 4

Although rillettes are typically made with meat or fish and some sort of fat and served in ramekins to be spread on toast points or baguette slices, there are renditions using mushrooms or onions or other vegetables, even lentils and walnuts, that I have found delicious.

Because I love the traditional French way of eating raw radishes with butter, radis au beurre, *on a baguette, I decided to blend the two concepts into one lovely little bowl of grated raw radishes mixed with butter to be spread on baguette slices. Use the best European-style butter or French butter you can buy.*

6 large radishes

8 ounces unsalted butter, at room temperature

$1/2$ teaspoon sea salt flakes, plus more for serving

French baguette slices or buttered toast points, for serving

If you buy radishes and are not going to use them right away, remove the greens, trim the stem and root, and scrub them clean. Place them in a zip-top bag layered with paper towel to keep them crisp until you use them.

When ready, grate the radishes on the large holes of a box grater.

Cut the butter into the bowl of a food processor and pulse to soften. Add the grated radishes and sea salt flakes and pulse until combined. You can finish the process, if you wish, in a bowl and stir the butter and radishes until blended. Pack the mixture into the ramekins of your choice and serve, or cover, refrigerate, and bring to room temperature before serving with baguette slices and a small bowl of sea salt flakes on the side.

Warm Tapenade Dip with Crudités

SERVES 4

A display of colorful vegetable finger food, like these crudités and their dip, is ideal for gatherings when you want to graze on something healthy and fresh, either as a light appetizer or on a buffet table.

Serve the tapenade, a Provençal specialty made predominantly with olives, warm in a butter warmer. It is worth buying a couple of warmers, as they are fun to use to melt chocolate to dip fruit into or warm butter for dipping shrimp or lobster, or to serve with these crudités. You can also use a fondue pot to keep the tapenade warm.

FOR THE VEGETABLES

4 asparagus spears, woody ends trimmed

4 celery stalks with leaves

8 radicchio leaves

8 Belgian endive leaves

2 red bell peppers, sliced

1 French baguette, sliced into dipping-size pieces

FOR THE TAPENADE

1 cup extra-virgin olive oil, divided

5 garlic cloves, minced, divided

1 (2-ounce) can anchovies preserved in olive oil, minced, oil reserved

1 cup Kalamata olives, pitted

1 tablespoon capers in brine, drained

$\frac{1}{4}$ cup minced fresh basil leaves

Grated zest of $\frac{1}{2}$ organic lemon

Juice of $\frac{1}{2}$ organic lemon

TO MAKE THE VEGETABLES: Arrange the vegetables on a large serving plate or cutting board. Add the baguette slices. Place a butter warmer or a fondue pot in the center of the arrangement.

TO MAKE THE TAPENADE: Pour $\frac{3}{4}$ cup of oil into a saucepan over medium heat. Add 3 minced garlic cloves, the anchovies, and the oil from the anchovy can. Cook for about 9 minutes, allowing the oil to boil and stirring with a wooden spoon as it cooks. Remove from the heat.

In the bowl of a food processor, combine the olives, capers, basil, lemon zest, lemon juice, and the remaining $\frac{1}{4}$ cup of oil and pulse 10 times. Add the remaining 2 minced garlic cloves and the anchovy-oil mixture and blend until smooth.

When ready to serve, heat the tapenade gently until warm, then transfer to the butter warmer for dipping.

Broccoli Terrine with Raw Tomato Sauce

SERVES 8 TO 9

Terrines are found all over France and are traditionally made in special earthenware baking pans, called "terrines," which look like loaf pans.

Terrines are typically made with chunky meats, but I also like to make terrines using vegetables. This fabulous light-as-air broccoli terrine is one of my favorite dishes to make in summer with the juicy raw tomato sauce served to its side. I prefer serving the terrine still warm, within a couple of hours of coming out of the oven, when the flavors are at their height; you can also serve it chilled, if you prefer.

FOR THE TERRINE

Unsalted butter, at room temperature, for the pan

2 pounds broccoli crowns

1 ½ teaspoons fine sea salt, plus more for the cooking water

6 large eggs, at room temperature

3 large egg whites, at room temperature

1 tablespoon Dijon mustard

½ teaspoon ground nutmeg

Dash cayenne pepper

1 cup whole milk

1 cup heavy cream

7 tablespoons grated Parmesan cheese

FOR THE SAUCE

1 ½ pounds tomatoes, unpeeled

2 garlic cloves, pressed

¼ cup extra-virgin olive oil

Juice of ½ organic lemon

¼ teaspoon sea salt, plus more to taste

½ cup fresh basil leaves, minced

TO MAKE THE TERRINE: Coat a 5 × 9-inch loaf pan generously with butter. Cut off a piece of parchment paper larger than the pan and fit it into the pan, letting it overhang the sides by a couple of inches at each end and pressing down on the bottoms and sides to flatten it.

Cut away the stems from the broccoli crowns, then break up the broccoli into very small florets. If you want to use part of the stems, slice them thinly, then cut into small dice.

Preheat the oven to 350 degrees F.

Bring a large saucepan full of water to a boil over high heat. Season the water generously with fine sea salt, then toss in the broccoli. Return to a boil, reduce the heat to maintain a simmer, and cook for 3 minutes. Drain, run the broccoli under cold water, then wrap the broccoli in paper towels and squeeze out any excess water until the broccoli is very dry. Toss the cooked broccoli into the prepared loaf pan, crumbling any large pieces with your hands so there are lots of little bits of broccoli.

In a bowl, whisk the eggs, egg whites, mustard, 1 ½ teaspoons fine sea salt, nutmeg, and cayenne until well blended. Pour in the milk and heavy cream and whisk to blend. Add the cheese and whisk to combine. Pour the liquid mixture over the broccoli.

Bake for 1 hour 30 minutes to 1 hour 35 minutes, or until a tester inserted into the center of the terrine comes out clean and the center is firm to the touch and dry. Remove from the oven and let cool for 10 minutes, then lift the broccoli terrine, using the parchment, onto a plate to completely cool.

TO MAKE THE SAUCE: Meanwhile, chop the tomatoes coarsely and toss into a blender or the bowl of a food processor. Add the garlic, oil, lemon juice, ¼ teaspoon sea salt, and the basil. Pulse a few times so you have mostly small pieces of tomato in the sauce. Taste and adjust the seasoning, then pour the sauce into a bowl.

If you are serving the terrine warm or at room temperature, cut it into 1-inch slices and place on plates. Use a slotted spoon to pick up only the tomatoes from the sauce, not the liquid, and ladle some of this over the slices to serve.

Grilled Brie with Apricots and Balsamic Glaze

SERVES 4

Who would think that cheese on the grill could taste so good? And paired with luscious fresh apricots, it is a surprising and delightful start to a casual meal. Don't be shy. Try it. It's a showstopper and utterly delicious.

3 tablespoons extra-virgin olive oil, divided

5 tablespoons honey, divided

4 fresh apricots, halved and pitted

1 (8-ounce) wheel Brie cheese

¼ cup store-bought balsamic glaze

French baguette slices, for serving

Preheat the grill to 450 degrees F, or a grill pan over high heat.

In a small pan over medium heat, heat 2 tablespoons of oil with 1 tablespoon of honey until the honey melts. Brush this mixture all over the apricot halves and put them on the grill, cut-side down. Cook for about 5 minutes until the apricots are nicely charred.

Coat the outside rind of the Brie wheel generously with the remaining 1 tablespoon of oil, place it on the hot grill, on the side away from the direct flame, close the grill lid, and cook for 2 minutes. Turn the cheese over, close the lid, and cook for 2 minutes. When the Brie is soft to the touch in the center, it is done.

Remove the Brie, quarter it, and place 1 quarter on each plate. Place 2 apricot halves next to the Brie, drizzle with the remaining 4 tablespoons of honey, and flick the balsamic glaze over the top in an attractive pattern. Serve with baguette slices.

Carrot and Zucchini Galettes with Red Caviar

SERVES 4

Galettes take all forms in France, from those that look like open pies to thin pancakes made with buckwheat flour to other types of pancakes holding a filling. This galette is a vegetable pancake that is crispy on the outside and soft on the inside. Around the holidays, I serve this with a spoonful of crème fraîche on top and budget-friendly red salmon caviar.

2 large eggs

1 tablespoon extra-virgin olive oil

²/₃ cup all-purpose flour

1 teaspoon fine sea salt

¹/₄ teaspoon ground cumin

2 cups shredded (on the large holes of a box grater) unpeeled zucchini (from about 2 medium)

2 cups shredded (on the large holes of a box grater) carrot (from about 1 large)

¹/₄ cup grated Parmesan cheese

1 teaspoon sugar

¹/₂ teaspoon baking powder

1 tablespoon unsalted butter

2 tablespoons extra-virgin olive oil

Coarse sea salt flakes

Crème fraîche or sour cream, for serving

Red salmon caviar, for serving

In a blender, combine the eggs, oil, flour, fine sea salt, and cumin and blend to combine. Let rest for 30 minutes.

Meanwhile, wrap the grated zucchini in paper towels and squeeze it over the sink to remove excess liquid. Transfer to a large bowl and add the carrot, Parmesan, and sugar. Stir well to mix.

Once the batter has rested for 30 minutes, add the baking powder and blend again to combine. Pour the batter over the vegetables in the bowl and mix well to coat.

In a large skillet over medium-high heat, melt the butter with the oil until sizzling, then turn the heat to medium. Working in batches as needed, drop in 3 tablespoons of the vegetable mixture for each galette, flattening each into a circle. Cook for 2 to 3 minutes per side until golden and crispy. Transfer to paper towels to drain while you cook the remaining galettes. Divide onto four plates.

Sprinkle with coarse sea salt and serve with a dollop of crème fraîche and caviar on each galette.

Alsatian Onion Crispbread
with Munster Cheese

SERVES 4

Tarte flambée, a much-loved treat in Alsace, in the north of France, is a large, usually rectangular, savory tart meant to be sliced and shared. The food even has an association called Confrérie du véritable Flammekueche *that promotes the authentic recipe—made with a thin, crisp crust without leavening and topped with thick cream, or crème fraîche, lardons, or little pieces of bacon, and onions that is then cooked, more often than not, in a wood oven—and suggests restaurants in Alsace where you can experience it. The recipe can vary from village to village, although a thin, crisp crust is always used. I've seen it done with crème fraîche and smoked salmon as well as a sweet version with apples and cinnamon sugar flambéed with Calvados.*

Rather than making that thin, crisp dough at home, I use store-bought puff pastry. And, in my version, I add grated Munster cheese, a lovely melting cheese from the Alsace region.

8 ounces smoked bacon

1 large yellow onion

2 tablespoons unsalted butter

2 teaspoons sugar

All-purpose flour, for dusting

1 sheet store-bought puff pastry

6 ounces crème fraîche or plain
   Greek-style yogurt

8 ounces mushrooms, sliced

Sea salt flakes

6 ounces Munster cheese, grated
   on the large holes of a box grater

Preheat the oven to 425 degrees F.

While the oven heats, slice the bacon into batons (small sticks) and transfer to a skillet over medium heat. Cook until the bacon is just beginning to crisp and has rendered most of its fat. Transfer to paper towels to drain. Wipe out the skillet with a paper towel.

Halve the onion, then very thinly slice the halves into half-moons. Separate the pieces into individual strands and toss them in a microwave-safe bowl. Barely cover the onion with water and let soak for 5 minutes, then drain and microwave, uncovered, for 1 minute. Drain and pat dry with paper towels.

Return the skillet to medium heat and add the butter to melt. Add the onions and sauté until lightly golden. Toward the end, sprinkle on the sugar and let cook to slightly caramelize the onions. Remove from the heat.

Place a 10 × 15-inch piece of parchment paper on a work surface, lightly dust it with flour, and place the pastry sheet on it. Roll the dough into a 10 × 15-inch rectangle. Loosely roll up the pastry, then unroll it onto a baking sheet.

Spread the crème fraîche thickly on the pastry sheet, leaving a ½-inch border along the edges. Scatter the onion pieces, bacon, and mushrooms over the top. Sprinkle with sea salt flakes, then distribute the cheese evenly over the top.

Bake for 10 to 20 minutes, or until the edges are crisp and golden brown. Timing will depend on how thin the dough is and the quantity of toppings on it. Begin taking a peek at 8 minutes. Carefully transfer to a cutting board, slice, and serve on the board.

Bistro Oeufs with Béarnaise Mayo Sauce

SERVES 4

This is one dish that brings a smile to my face when I see it on a menu. Old-fashioned yet still found in most French bistros and cafés. When it is good and served with excellent crusty bread, it is truly satisfying.

When I make it at home it is usually because I spied fresh-that-day free-range eggs at a farmers' market or roadside stand and immediately knew what I would make with them. Typically served on one or two leaves of lettuce, I also like to make it with a béarnaise mayo and garnish with two anchovy fillets on top in a crisscross pattern.

FOR THE MAYO

¼ cup white wine

¼ cup white or white balsamic vinegar

2 shallots, minced

2 tablespoons fresh tarragon leaves, minced, divided

Sea salt flakes

2 tablespoons freshly squeezed lemon juice

1 tablespoon Dijon mustard

2 large egg yolks

¾ cup extra-virgin olive oil

6 tablespoons store-bought mayonnaise

FOR SERVING

8 large hard-boiled eggs, peeled

8 large lettuce leaves

32 anchovy fillets (optional)

Crusty French baguette or thick sourdough bread slices, for serving

TO MAKE THE MAYO: Pour the wine and vinegar into a saucepan. Add the shallots, 1 tablespoon of tarragon, and 1 teaspoon of sea salt flakes and bring to a boil over high heat. Boil for 4 to 5 minutes until only about 2 tablespoons of liquid remain. Remove from the heat.

In the bowl of a food processor or a medium bowl, combine the lemon juice and mustard and mix. Add the egg yolks and process or whisk until well blended. With the machine running (or while whisking), slowly pour in the oil in a very thin stream until you have a thick mayonnaise consistency. Add the reduced vinegar mixture and the remaining 1 tablespoon of tarragon and pulse to combine. Add the store-bought mayonnaise and pulse to blend. Taste and season with more sea salt flakes, as needed. Refrigerate until ready to use.

TO SERVE: Halve each egg lengthwise. Spoon a small circle of béarnaise mayonnaise on each of 4 plates. Layer 2 lettuce leaves on the mayo on each plate, then arrange 4 egg halves in a daisy pattern on top of the lettuce. Spoon the remaining béarnaise mayonnaise over the eggs to completely cover them.

Cross 2 anchovy fillets (if using) on top of each egg half and serve with the crusty baguette.

Smoked Salmon and
Avocado Mousse in a Glass

SERVES 4

A longtime food trend in France that appears in homes as well as restaurants are verrines, *which are small glasses to hold either a starter, soup, or dessert.*

For this recipe, you will need four (about 6-ounce) verrines, glasses, or martini glasses to hold the appetizer. If you don't have the glasses, use small ramekins.

2 large ripe avocados, halved, pitted, and peeled

2 tablespoons freshly squeezed lemon juice

2 tablespoons extra-virgin olive oil

1/2 teaspoon sea salt flakes

3 tablespoons minced red onion

4 slices smoked salmon

6 tablespoons plain Greek-style yogurt

1 (5.2-ounce) package garlic and fines herbs Boursin cheese, at room temperature

4 tall, thin breadsticks (optional)

Slice the avocados into the bowl of a food processor. Add the lemon juice, oil, and sea salt flakes and process until smooth. Stir in the red onion. Divide the mousse among four serving glasses. Clean the food processor bowl.

Slice the smoked salmon into ribbons or cut it into small cubes. Top the avocado mixture with the salmon.

In the food processor, combine the yogurt and Boursin and blend until smooth. Alternately, use an immersion blender. Top each verrine with a layer of the yogurt mixture.

This can be eaten as is, or chilled before serving. Slide a breadstick (if using) into the side of each glass to garnish.

Grilled Cantaloupe Draped with Ham

SERVES 4

When I was a newlywed in Paris, my landlord taught me how to make a simple French dish that she always served to company. It was a wedge of sweet ripe Cavaillon melon with a thin slice of prosciutto on top. The key, she told me, was the quality of the ingredients. The melon had to taste like honey. The ham had to be paper-thin and salty and melt in your mouth. In my version, I grill the melon on a gas grill that has been sprayed with olive oil. It's a fun dish for backyard get-togethers.

Olive oil spray

1 ripe cantaloupe, quartered, peeled, and seeded

Extra-virgin olive oil, to coat the melon and to serve

Sea salt flakes

4 pieces thinly sliced ham

Preheat a grill to medium-high heat, or a grill pan over medium-high heat, and spray with olive oil.

Meanwhile, rub the melon quarters all over with a generous amount of oil.

When the grill is hot, place the melon pieces on the grill and cook for 1 to 2 minutes until the melon pieces are charred. Do not flip.

Put a melon wedge on each of four plates, drizzle with oil, and sprinkle with sea salt flakes to taste. Drape a slice of ham over each piece of melon to serve.

Small-Plate Tuna Confit Salade Niçoise

SERVES 4

To "confit" traditionally means to cook duck legs in duck fat. Another fat that you can "confit" with is olive oil, and you can confit almost anything.

For this flavorful small-plate salad, I like to slow-poach tuna in olive oil and serve it on a traditional salade niçoise. Although the authentic salade niçoise made in Nice requires canned tuna, not fresh, this dish sings a different note with fresh tuna confit.

FOR THE TUNA CONFIT

4 cups extra-virgin olive oil

6 garlic cloves, thinly sliced

5 thyme sprigs

1 pound best-quality raw tuna steak, at room temperature

FOR THE DRESSING

2 anchovy fillets

1 garlic clove, pressed or minced

¼ cup extra-virgin olive oil

1 tablespoon freshly squeezed lemon juice

FOR THE SALADE

4 cups mesclun

2 medium ripe tomatoes, quartered

½ small cucumber, thinly sliced

1 large hard-boiled egg, peeled and quartered

1 organic lemon, quartered

8 green or Kalamata olives, pitted

Extra-virgin olive oil, for drizzling

French baguette slices, for serving

TO MAKE THE TUNA CONFIT: In a Dutch oven or wide, deep skillet over medium-low heat, combine the oil, garlic, and thyme and heat until the oil reaches 160 degrees F.

Meanwhile, slice the tuna into 4 equal pieces and submerge them in the oil. Cover the pan and barely simmer for 5 to 12 minutes, depending on the thickness of the tuna and your preference for doneness. Slice into a piece to see if it is cooked through. Remove from the heat and let sit in the oil for 3 minutes, then use a slotted spoon to transfer the tuna to paper towel to drain.

TO MAKE THE DRESSING: Put the anchovy fillets in a large bowl and mash with a fork. Add the garlic, oil, and lemon juice and whisk to combine.

TO MAKE THE SALADE: Toss the mesclun into the bowl with the dressing and, with clean hands, "massage" the dressing into the leaves. Divide the greens among four plates. Place a piece of tuna on each mound of greens. To the side of each, add a tomato quarter, cucumber slices, a hard-boiled egg quarter, a lemon quarter, and 2 olives. Drizzle a little oil over the tuna and serve with the baguette slices to the side.

Crêpes with Ham, Cheese, Tomato, and Egg

SERVES 4

When I want to save time, I use store-bought dessert crêpes, which are easily found, usually near the berries or in the fruit section of a grocery store.

In summer, when ripe tomatoes are available, this makes a quick and delicious appetizer or light lunch. The slight sweetness of the crêpes plays well against the salty ham and cheese. Use any cheese that melts well.

4 store-bought crêpes

2 tablespoons Dijon mustard

4 slices ham

4 slices cheese of choice

2 large ripe tomatoes, thickly sliced

2 tablespoons unsalted butter

4 large eggs, at room temperature

Preheat the oven to 350 degrees F. Line a baking sheet with parchment paper.

Lay the crêpes on the prepared baking sheet and lightly brush each one with mustard. Top each with a slice of ham, then a slice of cheese, then a slice of tomato. Fold down the top of the crêpe, the bottom up, and each side in toward the middle so you can still see a little bit of the tomato.

Bake for 10 minutes, or until the cheese is melted.

Meanwhile, in a large nonstick skillet over medium heat, melt the butter. Crack the eggs into the skillet and fry them until they have reached the level of doneness you prefer.

Remove the crêpes from the oven, put one on each plate, then top each in the center with a fried egg to serve.

SOUPS

Hot soup has its warming presence that starts a cold evening well, while an interesting cold soup has everyone's anticipation piqued at what comes next, both a great way to start a meal.

I have a habit of having a pot of soup simmering at the back of my stove most days. I might throw in leftovers from the night before, something I picked in the garden that morning, add a bit of rice, a splash of wine, some herbs I picked along the road. It's a delicious treat on a drizzly Saturday, or for later when I may be too tired to cook a full meal.

If I have time, I make a lovely stock to start. But since most of the French I know reach for a chicken or beef bouillon cube, I do the same and admit to preferring the flavor compared to bland boxed or canned broths. In the following recipes, where it lists chicken, beef, or vegetable broth, I suggest making it with cubes according to the package instructions, unless you have homemade stock.

Some of the soups that follow are hearty enough to be a main course, whereas others can be a first course.

Sheet Pan Butternut Squash and Apple Soup

SERVES 4

You just roast everything at once on a sheet pan to make this soup, an autumn or winter blend of butternut squash and sweet apples with a hint of fresh sage as a garnish. It all happens in the oven where the flavors intensify, then a quick whir in the food processor and it's ready to serve.

FOR THE SOUP

1 butternut squash

Extra-virgin olive oil, for coating the squash

1 medium white onion, unpeeled

2 sweet apples

1 ½ cups chicken broth

2 teaspoons fine sea salt

5 tablespoons packed light brown sugar

2 tablespoons unsalted butter

FOR THE GARNISH

4 tablespoons plain Greek-style yogurt

2 teaspoons fine sea salt

4 fresh sage leaves, minced

Preheat the oven to 425 degrees F.

TO MAKE THE SOUP: Wash and pat dry the squash. Leaving the skin on, halve it vertically. Leave the seeds in the squash. Using oil, lightly coat the squash all over, then place it on a rimmed sheet pan, cut-side down. Put the whole onion, skin on, on the sheet pan.

Bake for 20 minutes.

Add the apples to the sheet pan and bake for 25 to 30 minutes, or until the squash is very tender. Remove from the oven and let the vegetables and apples cool enough for you to work with them.

Turn the squash over and use a spoon to remove and discard the seeds. Scoop out the flesh and put it in the bowl of a food processor. Core the apples and put the flesh into the food processor. Squeeze the flesh from the onion into the food processor. Discard the peel. Pour in the broth, add the fine sea salt and brown sugar, and blend until very smooth and light. Pour the soup into a saucepan and warm over medium heat.

TO MAKE THE GARNISH: In a small bowl, whisk the yogurt and fine sea salt to blend.

TO SERVE: Divide the soup among four bowls and garnish each serving with minced sage leaves in the center and a swirl of the salted yogurt to one side of the bowl.

Provençal Vegetable Soup with Pistou

SERVES 8

I absolutely love making this soup now that I have figured out how to make it using my food processor. It used to be quite labor-intensive to cut all the vegetables by hand. Now, I just throw them into the food processor to chop into small pieces, then toss them into my Dutch oven. So quick, so simple, and I also vastly prefer the texture of the soup prepared this way to the traditional way I was taught to make it. The vegetables don't all come out the same perfect size, which I like, and the rice or pasta is cooked at the same time, making it possible to get my soup on the table pretty quickly.

You can, literally, put any vegetables in soupe au pistou. In spring, I add asparagus and loads of fresh peas. In summer, more ripe tomatoes. In fall, I add butternut squash. It is a substantial soup, and served with a baguette, it could easily be the meal's main course. A green salad is a nice accompaniment.

FOR THE SOUP

1 medium leek

3 tablespoons extra-virgin olive oil

2 green bell peppers, seeded and quartered

1 large carrot, cut into chunks

2 medium potatoes, peeled and cut into chunks

1 medium zucchini, unpeeled, cut into chunks

5 ounces green beans, trimmed and cut into 1-inch pieces

2 ounces basmati rice, rinsed, or small pasta (such as orzo)

3 bay leaves

2 teaspoons minced fresh rosemary leaves

3 thyme sprigs

1 $\frac{1}{2}$ teaspoons sea salt, plus more to taste

6 cups water or chicken stock

4 medium tomatoes, finely chopped, keeping seeds and juice

1 (15.5-ounce) can cannellini beans, drained and rinsed

TO MAKE THE SOUP: Slice off the dark green part of the leek (save for another use or compost) and use only the white and very light green parts. Trim off the root end, then halve the leek vertically. Rinse the leek under running water to wash away any sand or dirt. Cut the leek into chunks.

In a Dutch oven or soup pot over low heat, warm the oil.

Toss the leek into a food processor and pulse 6 times until it becomes small pieces, then transfer to the pot. Do the same with the bell peppers, until they are very small chunks. Pulse the carrot 7 times (it's okay if the carrot pieces are uneven sizes), then the potatoes 7 times, and add the vegetables to the pot. Pulse the zucchini 6 times so there will be some bigger pieces and toss into the pot.

Add the green beans, rice, bay leaves, rosemary, thyme, and 1 $\frac{1}{2}$ teaspoons sea salt. Pour in the water and bring to a boil over high heat. Once boiling, reduce the heat to maintain a simmer and cook for 15 to 20 minutes until the vegetables are cooked to your liking. Remove and discard the bay leaves and thyme sprigs.

Stir in the tomatoes, with their seeds and juice, as well as the cannellini beans. Taste the soup and add more sea salt, as needed.

continued >>

2 cups tightly packed fresh basil
leaves

3 garlic cloves, sliced into thirds

¼ teaspoon sea salt

¼ cup extra-virgin olive oil, plus
more as needed

3 tablespoons freshly grated
Parmesan cheese

FOR THE GARNISH

1 cup freshly grated Emmental
cheese

1 small bunch fresh parsley, leaves
only, minced

Good extra-virgin olive oil, for
drizzling

TO MAKE THE PISTOU: When the soup is ready, in the bowl of a food processor, combine the basil, garlic, and sea salt and process until combined. With the machine running, drizzle in the oil until the pistou becomes a spreadable paste. Transfer to a small bowl and whisk in the Parmesan.

TO SERVE AND GARNISH: Ladle the hot soup into bowls. Place a spoonful of the pistou into the center of the soup in each bowl. Sprinkle a bit of grated Emmental and minced parsley over the top and drizzle with a little oil.

Three-Cheese French Onion Soup

SERVES 4

I was introduced to French onion soup as a young child when my father took us to Les Halles and Au Pied de Cochon restaurant when we were in Paris on vacation to experience it. All these years, I have gone back and back to relive dipping my spoon into that soup.

When I am hit with a mood of nostalgia, especially in winter around the holidays, I make this recipe. Traditionally made with a rich beef broth, I make mine with chicken broth and add a little extra cheese!

2 large yellow onions

2 large red onions

2 tablespoons unsalted butter, at room temperature

2 tablespoons extra-virgin olive oil

2 teaspoons granulated sugar

1 teaspoon light brown sugar

2 teaspoons all-purpose flour

4 cups chicken stock

$\frac{1}{2}$ teaspoon fine sea salt

1 teaspoon Dijon mustard

2 thyme sprigs, leaves only

2 tablespoons Cognac

4 (1-inch-thick) sourdough baguette slices

$\frac{1}{2}$ cup grated Gruyère cheese

$\frac{1}{4}$ cup grated Munster cheese

$\frac{1}{4}$ cup grated Emmental cheese

Halve the yellow and red onions, then halve them again. Cut the onions pieces into $\frac{1}{2}$-inch-thick slices.

In a Dutch oven or heavy soup pot over medium-low heat, melt the butter. Add the oil, then all of the onions, and cook very slowly, for about 20 minutes, or longer, until they take on a deep brown color. Turn the heat to medium-high and sprinkle in the granulated and brown sugars. Cook for 1 minute to caramelize the onions. Remove from the heat, sprinkle in the flour, and stir well to coat the onions.

Pour in the stock, return the pot to medium-high heat, and bring to a boil. Reduce the heat to maintain a simmer and stir in the fine sea salt, mustard, thyme, and Cognac. Keep the soup on a low simmer.

Preheat the broiler.

Place the baguette slices on a baking sheet, divide the Gruyère, Munster, and Emmental cheeses over the top of the bread slices and broil, watching carefully, until the cheese is melted and bubbly.

Ladle the soup into four bowls and top with a baguette slice to serve.

Chilled Summer Tomato Soup with Soft Garlic Breadcrumbs

SERVES 4

It seems counter intuitive to pair a cold soup with breadcrumbs on top, but that lovely addition just melts into every wonderful mouthful. The breadcrumbs are not baked so they are soft and delicious little flavor bombs. This soup is at its best when you use really sweet, ripe summer tomatoes.

FOR THE BREADCRUMBS

4 slices white bread, crusts removed, quartered

$\frac{1}{4}$ teaspoon fine sea salt

3 garlic cloves, sliced

3 tablespoons extra-virgin olive oil

FOR THE SOUP

2 medium shallots, chopped

2 large garlic cloves, chopped

1 $\frac{1}{2}$ teaspoons sea salt flakes

$\frac{1}{4}$ cup extra-virgin olive oil

2 slices white bread, crusts removed, diced

2 tablespoons whole milk

2 teaspoons sugar

1 tablespoon herbes de Provence

2 pounds sweetest ripe tomatoes, unpeeled, chopped, keeping the seeds and juice

2 tablespoons minced fresh basil leaves

TO MAKE THE BREADCRUMBS: In the bowl of a food processor, combine the bread, fine sea salt, and garlic and process until coarse crumbs form. With the machine running, stream in the oil until combined. Set aside.

TO MAKE THE SOUP: In a blender, combine the shallots, garlic, sea salt flakes, oil, bread, milk, sugar, herbes de Provence, and tomatoes, along with their seeds and juice. Blend the soup until very smooth. Chill until ready to use.

Divide the soup among four bowls and mound breadcrumbs in the middle. Sprinkle with the minced basil to garnish.

Chilled Velvety Avocado
and Swiss Chard Soup

This soup has a smooth, light consistency that delivers mouthfeel as well as delicious flavor from the marriage of avocado and Swiss chard. It has become my go-to company soup, it's so good. Refrigerate for 3 hours before serving. Chill the garnishes as well.

FOR THE SOUP

3 avocados

¼ cup freshly squeezed lime juice (from 2 limes)

3 large garlic cloves, halved

1 ½ large cucumbers, peeled and cut into 2-inch chunks

1 cup tightly packed coarsely chopped Swiss chard leaves

3 tablespoons extra-virgin olive oil

1 cup water

1 cup plain Greek-style yogurt

1 teaspoon fine sea salt, plus more as needed

FOR THE GARNISH

1 avocado

1 medium firm tomato, cut into small dice

2 scallions, thinly sliced

Coarse sea salt flakes

Balsamic vinegar, for drizzling

TO MAKE THE SOUP: Coarsely chop the avocados and toss into the bowl of a food processor.

Add the lime juice, garlic, cucumbers, chard, oil, water, yogurt, and fine sea salt and process until smooth. Taste and add more salt, as needed. Transfer the soup to a bowl, cover, and refrigerate for 3 hours.

TO MAKE THE GARNISH: Just before serving, halve, pit, peel, and cut the avocado into small dice. Divide the avocado into the center of four bowls and gently ladle the soup over it. Garnish with the diced tomato and sliced scallions, then sprinkle a few coarse sea salt flakes over the scallions. Swirl a thin line of vinegar around the garnish to serve.

Turnip Soup from the Île-de-France

SERVES 4

There are hundreds of varieties of turnips grown in the Île-de-France region north of Paris and, more often than not, they turn up in soup. My soup tastes earthy and slightly sweet, proving just how delicious the lowly turnip can be.

2 tablespoons extra-virgin olive oil

1 medium white onion, thinly sliced

4 large garlic cloves, minced

3 turnips, peeled and coarsely chopped

1 large Yukon gold potato, peeled and coarsely chopped

4 cups chicken broth or vegetable broth

1 thyme sprig, leaves only

1 tablespoon light brown sugar

$\frac{1}{2}$ teaspoon fine sea salt, plus more as needed

$\frac{1}{4}$ cup half-and-half

Freshly ground black pepper (optional)

In a large Dutch oven or saucepan over medium heat, heat the oil. Add the onion and garlic and cook for 5 minutes. Add the turnips, potato, broth, thyme, brown sugar, and fine sea salt. Bring to a boil, then reduce the heat to maintain a simmer. Cook for 30 minutes until the vegetables are very tender.

Working in batches as needed, transfer the soup to a blender or the bowl of a food processor and blend until smooth. Add the half-and-half and blend again. Taste and add more fine sea salt and some pepper, as needed. Serve hot.

Carrot and Cauliflower Soup

The delicate color and the hint of Parmesan cheese make this a more interesting soup than it sounds. It can be quite elegant, served in a good china bowl on a snowy evening.

4 tablespoons extra-virgin olive oil, divided, plus more for drizzling

1 medium white onion, chopped

1 pound carrots, cut into ½-inch pieces

6 cups water or chicken broth

1 head cauliflower, chopped into small pieces

Grated zest of 1 organic lemon

Juice of 1 organic lemon

1 ½ cups grated Parmesan cheese, divided

1 tablespoon sea salt flakes, plus more to taste

In a Dutch oven or large saucepan over medium heat, heat 2 tablespoons of oil. Add the onion and cook until translucent. Add the carrots and water and bring to a boil over high heat. Reduce the heat to maintain a simmer and cook for 10 minutes.

Add the cauliflower, cover the pot, and simmer for 25 minutes, or until all the vegetables are soft. Remove from the heat and let cool for 5 to 10 minutes, then transfer to a blender in batches to purée until smooth. To the last batch, add the remaining 2 tablespoons of oil when puréeing, then pour the soup back into the Dutch oven and stir to blend.

Stir in the lemon zest, lemon juice, and 1 cup of Parmesan. Add 1 tablespoon of sea salt flakes, taste, and add more sea salt flakes, as needed, before serving. Drizzle a little oil over the soup and sprinkle with some of the remaining Parmesan.

Clear Fish Soup
with Mussels and Scallops

SERVES 4

This is a soup happily eaten as a main course with great bread and a salad. The trick here is using both the broth from cooking the mussels and bottled clam juice for the soup base, which produces a flavorful canvas for the fish. Somehow it works.

The most popular French fish soups, bouillabaisse and soupe de poisson, *are served with a* rouille, *a garlicy derivative of mayonnaise, which is spread onto toasted baguette slices that float on top of the hot soup. I have included a recipe for home-made rouille, but if you don't want to consume raw egg, simply use 1 cup store-bought mayonnaise instead of the egg yolks and olive oil and blend it with the rest of the rouille ingredients.*

FOR THE ROUILLE

2 large egg yolks, at room
   temperature

3 garlic cloves, sliced

½ jarred roasted red bell pepper

1 tablespoon freshly squeezed
   lemon juice

½ teaspoon fine sea salt

¼ teaspoon sweet paprika

Dash cayenne pepper

½ cup extra-virgin olive oil, plus
   more as needed

TO MAKE THE ROUILLE: In the bowl of a food processor or a blender, combine the egg yolks, garlic, roasted red pepper, lemon juice, fine sea salt, paprika, and cayenne and process until smooth. With the machine running, drizzle in the oil in a thin stream until the mixture has the consistency of mayonnaise. Transfer to a bowl, cover, and refrigerate until ready to use.

continued >>

FOR THE SOUP

1 medium leek

20 large mussels

2 cups dry white wine, divided

4 small potatoes, unpeeled, halved

1 medium onion, diced

4 garlic cloves, minced

1 medium carrot, grated

3 thyme sprigs, or 2 teaspoons dried leaves

2 bay leaves

3 cups bottled clam juice

$\frac{1}{2}$ teaspoon fine sea salt

2 cups cubed firm white fish (such as cod or monkfish)

8 large sea scallops, halved

8 French baguette slices, toasted

$\frac{1}{4}$ cup minced fresh flat-leaf parsley leaves

TO MAKE THE SOUP: Slice off the dark green part of the leek (save for another use or compost) and use only the white and very light green parts. Trim off the root end, then halve the leek vertically. Rinse the leek under running water to wash away any sand or dirt. Thinly slice the leek.

Scrub the mussels under running water, pulling off and discarding any beards. Discard any mussels that do not close when you tap them on the counter, or any that are damaged. I've added a few extras in case you need to throw some away. Place the mussels in a Dutch oven or large soup pot and pour in 1 cup of wine.

Place the pot over medium heat, cover it, and cook for about 5 minutes. Watch carefully as you want to take the mussels off the heat as soon as they open. Using a slotted spoon, transfer the mussels to a bowl, leaving the mussel broth in the pot. Discard any mussels that did not open after being cooked.

In a medium saucepan, combine the potatoes with enough water to cover and bring to a boil over high heat. Once boiling, reduce the heat to maintain a simmer and cook until fork-tender. Using a slotted spoon, transfer to a plate and keep warm with a tent of aluminum foil.

Add the onion, garlic, leek, carrot, thyme, bay leaves, clam juice, remaining 1 cup of wine, and fine sea salt to the mussel broth in the pot. Simmer until the vegetables are tender.

Add the fish and scallops and simmer for 3 to 4 minutes, or until the fish is opaque and cooked through. Add the reserved mussels and the reserved potatoes and simmer for another minute to warm. Remove and discard the bay leaves and thyme sprigs.

Serve the soup in bowls. Spread the rouille onto the toasted baguette slices and float two in each bowl. Scatter the minced parsley over the top.

Creamless Cream of Mushroom Soup

SERVES 4

Mad for mushrooms? This soup gets its powerhouse flavor from buttery sautéed mushrooms with fresh herbs. Mushroom soup served in France is normally luxuriously rich, made with heavy cream and egg yolks and a base of béchamel. In my version, I start by making duxelles, *finely chopped mushrooms sautéed in butter, and my base for the soup is a béchamel sauce made with milk. No cream or eggs, yet it is deliciously satisfying.*

1 ½ pounds button mushrooms, rinsed and trimmed

2 medium shallots, quartered

4 tablespoons unsalted butter, divided

1 thyme sprig, leaves only, or ½ teaspoon dried leaves

1 teaspoon fine sea salt

Freshly ground black pepper

¼ cup all-purpose flour

1 ½ cups chicken broth

2 cups whole milk

1 tablespoon extra-virgin olive oil

8 ounces baby bella mushrooms, thickly sliced

Coarse sea salt flakes

1 to 2 tablespoons dry sherry (optional)

¼ cup fresh flat-leaf parsley leaves, minced

In two batches, toss the button mushrooms directly into the bowl of a food processor, including their stems, and pulse about 10 times, just until finely chopped. Transfer to a large bowl.

Toss the shallots into the bowl of the food processor and pulse 10 times until finely chopped. Transfer to the bowl with the button mushrooms. It will look like a lot of mushrooms and shallots but they will cook down.

In a Dutch oven or large deep skillet over medium heat, melt 2 tablespoons of butter, then add the button mushrooms and shallots, and thyme. Cook for 3 minutes. Sprinkle in the fine sea salt and pepper to taste. Cook the mushrooms slowly for 8 minutes, letting them cook down while bubbling around the edges, stirring frequently. Remove from the heat.

In a saucepan over medium heat, melt the remaining 2 tablespoons of butter. Sprinkle in the flour and cook, whisking, for 2 minutes. Pour in 1 cup of broth and whisk until smooth, then add the remaining ½ cup of broth and the milk. Increase the heat to medium-high and cook for about 4 minutes, whisking well to combine, until bubbling and thickened. Remove from the heat.

Transfer the cooked mushroom mixture to the food processor and blend until smooth. Pour the mushrooms into the sauce, whisk, and keep warm over low heat.

In a skillet over medium-high heat, heat the oil until it shimmers, then toss in the baby bella mushrooms and cook them quickly, until golden. Transfer to a paper towel and sprinkle with the coarse sea salt.

To serve, reheat the soup to a simmer, stir in the sherry (if using), then ladle the soup into four bowls. Garnish with the baby bella slices and a sprinkle of minced parsley. Grind some pepper over the top of each and serve.

Watercress and Scallion Vichyssoise

SERVES 4

Although vichyssoise is not French, it was conceptualized in America around a classic French potato and leek soup that is served hot. Vichyssoise is served cold and is really refreshing.

I've taken the basic recipe and added watercress and scallions to it; alternatively, you could add asparagus, fresh peas, or cauliflower and cook them at the same time as the potatoes and leeks. Then purée and chill. Et voilà!

2 medium leeks

5 Yukon gold potatoes, unpeeled, thinly sliced

5 cups chicken broth

1 teaspoon sea salt

$\frac{1}{4}$ teaspoon ground nutmeg

$\frac{1}{4}$ teaspoon ground white pepper

1 bunch fresh watercress, roots trimmed, rinsed, and dried

$\frac{1}{2}$ cup heavy (whipping) cream

4 scallions, trimmed and finely sliced

4 tablespoons minced fresh chives

Slice off the dark green part of the leeks (save for another use or compost) and use only the white and very light green parts. Trim off the root ends, then halve the leeks vertically. Rinse the leeks under running water to wash away any sand or dirt. Cut the leeks into 1-inch pieces and toss them into a soup pot.

Add the potatoes, broth, sea salt, nutmeg, and pepper to the pot and bring to a boil over high heat. Reduce the heat to maintain a simmer and cook for 25 to 30 minutes, or until the vegetables are fork-tender. Turn off the heat and let the soup cool to room temperature.

Working in batches as needed, transfer the cooled soup to the bowl of a food processor or a blender and process until smooth. Add the watercress, stems and all, and process until smooth. Transfer to a large bowl, cover, and refrigerate for at least 3 hours.

When ready to serve, in a medium bowl and using a handheld electric mixer, whip the heavy cream on high speed to almost stiff peaks, then fold it gently into the chilled soup, using a whisk at the end if needed to blend more thoroughly. Ladle the soup into bowls and top each serving with 1 tablespoon of sliced scallions and 1 tablespoon of minced chives.

Fresh Spring Pea Soup with Mint

SERVES 6

The origin of this classic French soup, called potage Saint-Germain, *is often tied to the court of King Louis XIV. This version is a fresh pea soup made with lettuce and mint, an intriguing combination.*

1 leek

2 tablespoons unsalted butter

4 cups chopped romaine lettuce

1 large shallot, finely chopped

3 cups vegetable stock or chicken stock

1 medium Yukon gold potato, peeled and cut into small dice

4 cups fresh peas, divided

2 tablespoons extra-virgin olive oil

2 flat-leaf parsley sprigs, chopped

16 fresh mint leaves, chopped

1 teaspoon sea salt

1 ½ cups water

8 fresh mint leaves, finely chopped, plus more to garnish

4 red radicchio leaves, thinly sliced

Slice off the dark green part of the leek (save for another use or compost) and use only the white and very light green parts. Trim off the root end, then halve the leek vertically. Rinse the leek under running water to wash away any sand or dirt. Thinly slice the leek.

In a large saucepan over medium heat, melt the butter. Add the lettuce, leek, and shallot and cook until soft. Pour in the stock, add the potato and 3 cups of peas, and simmer until the potatoes and peas are soft.

Working in batches as needed, transfer the soup to a blender, add the oil, parsley, and mint and blend until very smooth. Pour the soup into the saucepan and whisk in the sea salt.

In another medium saucepan over medium heat, combine the water and remaining 1 cup of peas. Simmer and cook, adjusting the temperature as needed, until the peas are just soft. Drain and add the whole peas into the puréed soup.

Serve in bowls garnished with a scattering of chopped mint leaves and the sliced radicchio.

Laughing Cow Zucchini Soup

SERVES 4

The grandfather of a friend used to make this soup for his lunch. I was fascinated watching him unwrap wedges of Laughing Cow cheese at the end of making his soup to add a creaminess to the blend. It works.

2 tablespoons extra-virgin olive oil

2 garlic cloves, thinly sliced

2 medium zucchini, unpeeled, ends trimmed

2 red or Yukon gold potatoes, peeled and cut into small dice

3 ½ cups water

1 ½ teaspoons sea salt flakes

Freshly ground black pepper

3 Laughing Cow cheese wedges, of choice

In a soup pot over medium heat, heat the oil. Add the garlic and cook for 3 minutes.

Halve the zucchini vertically, then cut it crosswise into half-moons. Add the zucchini to the pot, along with the potatoes. Cook for 4 minutes, stirring frequently.

Pour in the water, bring to a boil over high heat, then reduce the heat to maintain a simmer. Cover the pot and cook for about 20 minutes until the zucchini and potatoes are very tender.

Working in two batches, transfer the soup to a blender or food processor and process until silky smooth. To the last batch, add the sea salt flakes and pepper to taste. Crumble in the cheese and blend until smooth. Pour the soup back into the pot, stir, and reheat over medium heat until hot. Ladle into soup bowls to serve.

SALADS

Les salades are either very simple or more complex and composed of several elements.

For me, if I have fresh in-season lettuce that I have gently massaged with a fabulous mustard vinaigrette, I am in heaven. I always serve a salad with baguette slices to soak up the vinaigrette.

I think of a composed salad, *salade composée*, as more of a light meal. For instance, my Red and Yellow Roasted Beet, Goat Cheese, and Walnut Salad (page 79), is a substantial salad perfect for lunch.

French from the Market Taboulé

SERVES 6 TO 8

One of my favorite salads found all over France, in markets, restaurants, and premade in grocery stores, is taboulé, *which is predominantly green from an abundance of parsley, with a bit of couscous thrown in.*

I like to use half curly-leaf parsley with the traditional flat-leaf parsley because it tends to add loft and fluffiness to the salad. And although many recipes call for firm tomatoes, minus their juice, I prefer ripe, sweet tomatoes for their wonderful flavor and I treasure their juice and greedily save it to add to my salad.

Unlike other salads, taboulé admirably holds its own for the next two days so it is a great way to start a weekend and have some leftovers to enjoy with other meals.

1 cup dried couscous

5 ripe tomatoes

1 medium cucumber, peeled

1 bunch fresh flat-leaf parsley, rinsed and dried

1 bunch fresh curly-leaf parsley, rinsed and dried

¼ cup extra-virgin olive oil

Juice of 1 ½ organic lemons, plus more as needed

1 teaspoon sea salt, plus more as needed

Cook the couscous according to the package instructions. Fluff with a fork, transfer to a bowl, and let come to room temperature.

Meanwhile, thinly slice the tomatoes, stack the slices, and cut them into bâtons (sticks), then turn and cut the sticks into small dice, saving the juice. Toss the diced tomatoes and their juice into a large bowl.

Thinly slice the cucumber, stack the slices, and cut them into small cubes. Toss into the bowl with the tomatoes.

Lay a box grater on its side with the large holes facing up. Pull the flat-leaf and curly-leaf parsley, stem by stem, through the large holes of the grater to pull off the leaves and toss the leaves into the bowl of a food processor. Save the stems for another use. Pulse the leaves 10 times to finely chop and transfer them to the bowl with the vegetables. Stir to combine.

Stir in the cooked couscous to combine.

In a small bowl, whisk the oil, lemon juice, and sea salt to combine. Pour the dressing over the salad and mix well to coat and combine. Taste and add more lemon juice or sea salt, as needed.

Refrigerate for 30 minutes before serving.

Frisée Salad with Roquefort Toasts

SERVES 4

A frilly, lacy lettuce, frisée is a variety of endive/chicory, having the same slightly bitter flavor. Its origins are believed to date back to ancient Egypt. For many of us, it is a welcome sight at most restaurants and cafés in France in the form of the salade frisée aux lardons, *which is presented with a poached egg on top, and makes a wonderful lunch with, of course, baguette slices and a glass of wine!*

With this version, I dress the frisée salad simply and complement it with the fabulous Roquefort cheese, the slightly strong blue cheese from Roquefort-sur-Soulzon in the South of France, on toasts presented to the side.

8 cups frisée lettuce, rinsed and dried

1 cup finely sliced radicchio leaves

1 tablespoon finely minced shallot

2 tablespoons white wine vinegar

2 teaspoons Dijon mustard, plus more as needed

Freshly ground black pepper

6 tablespoons extra-virgin olive oil

Sea salt, as needed

8 French baguette slices

8 ounces Roquefort cheese, at room temperature

Preheat the broiler.

In a large bowl, toss together the frisée and radicchio.

In small bowl, stir together the shallot and vinegar, then let the mixture rest for 5 minutes. Add the mustard and pepper to taste and whisk to blend. While whisking, slowly drizzle in the oil until well blended. Taste and add sea salt or more mustard, as needed.

Place the baguette slices on a baking sheet and toast under the broiler, watching carefully, until just golden.

In another small bowl, use a fork to mash the cheese a bit to soften it up. Spread the cheese onto the toast slices.

Pour the dressing onto the salad and, with clean hands, gently massage the vinaigrette into the leaves. Arrange the salad on four plates and add 2 Roquefort toasts to each plate to serve.

Arugula Salad over Watermelon with Herbed Goat Cheese

To be served as a surprise, this looks like an arugula salad, but when you dig in, there is a juicy wedge of sweet watermelon underneath that is a lovely counterpoint to the salty salad and cheese above.

FOR THE HERBED CHEESE

2 tablespoons minced fresh oregano leaves

2 tablespoons minced fresh basil leaves

¼ teaspoon sea salt

1 (11-ounce) log soft goat cheese

FOR THE DRESSING

¼ cup extra-virgin olive oil

Juice of ½ organic lemon

¼ teaspoon Dijon mustard

¼ teaspoon fine sea salt, plus more as needed

FOR THE SALAD

1 (1-inch-thick) slice small watermelon, cut into 4 triangles

2 bunches fresh arugula, rinsed and dried

TO MAKE THE HERBED CHEESE: In a medium bowl, stir together the oregano, basil, and sea salt to combine. Crumble in the goat cheese and, using a fork, mash everything together to combine. Tear off a large piece of plastic wrap. Spoon the goat cheese mixture into the center and re-form it into a log. Wrap in the plastic and refrigerate until ready to serve.

TO MAKE THE DRESSING: In a large bowl, whisk the oil, lemon juice, mustard, and fine sea salt to blend. Taste and add more fine sea salt, as needed.

TO MAKE THE SALAD: Place one watermelon triangle on each of four plates. Add the arugula to the dressing and toss to coat and combine, then heap the arugula on top of each watermelon slice to hide it. Slice or crumble the herbed goat cheese on top to serve.

Spinach Mimosa Salad

Outside of my house in the South of France I had a couple of mimosa trees. When they bloomed, beginning in January, they were covered with masses of buttery-yellow fragrant flowers that I would gather in great bunches to bring into the house to cheer up winter's gray light. The term "mimosa," in French cooking, refers to using finely grated egg yolks to mimic the look of the beautiful little yellow mimosa flowers from the mimosa tree.

FOR THE VINAIGRETTE

1/3 cup extra-virgin olive oil

2 tablespoons freshly squeezed lemon juice

1 tablespoon white or white wine vinegar

2 teaspoons Dijon mustard

1 garlic clove, pressed or minced

1/4 teaspoon fine sea salt

FOR THE SALAD

1 pound fresh spinach leaves

1 red bell pepper, thinly sliced

1 yellow bell pepper, thinly sliced

2 radishes, very thinly sliced

1 medium shallot, thinly sliced and separated into rings

8 ounces mushrooms, thickly sliced

2 scallions, white part only, thinly sliced

6 large hard-boiled eggs, chilled, and peeled

1/4 cup finely minced fresh chives or dill fronds

TO MAKE THE VINAIGRETTE: In a small bowl, whisk the oil, lemon juice, vinegar, mustard, garlic, and fine sea salt to blend. Set aside.

TO MAKE THE SALAD: In a large bowl, toss together the spinach, red and yellow bell peppers, radishes, shallot, mushrooms, and scallions. Pour in the vinaigrette and, with clean hands, gently massage it into the salad ingredients so they are well coated. Divide the salad among four plates or shallow bowls.

Separate the egg whites from the yolks. Rub the whites over the large holes of a box grater right over the salad greens on each plate. Rub the yolks over the large holes of the grater on top of the whites. Sprinkle with the minced chives and serve.

Red and White Endive and Apple Salad with Crispy Lardons

SERVES 4

Crunchy and bitter, this two-color endive salad can hold its own at a sophisticated dinner party, where you can tell them the story of how endive was discovered. The story goes that a farmer in Belgium went to check on his chicory roots in the cellar and found these funny cylindrical leaves growing on them. Ever frugal, he decided they would make a good vegetable to eat. That was in 1830, so it is a relatively new vegetable that the French took to. One of my favorite ways to use it is in endives au jambon, *endives that are rolled in a slice of ham and baked in lots of cheesy Mornay sauce. Here, I present them to you in a beautiful salad.*

6 ounces bacon

1 tablespoon finely minced shallot

2 tablespoons white vinegar

1 teaspoon Dijon mustard

6 tablespoons extra-virgin olive oil

3 red endives

3 white endives

1 small Granny Smith apple, peeled

Slice the bacon into matchsticks. These are your "lardons." In a skillet over medium heat, cook the lardons until crispy. Transfer to paper towel to drain and reserve.

In a small bowl, combine the shallot and vinegar and let rest for 10 minutes. Whisk in the mustard and, while whisking, drizzle in the oil until the vinaigrette is well blended.

Pull off any outer leaves on the endives that may be brown. Slice off the ends, then slice the endives into $\frac{1}{2}$-inch pieces and toss them into a large bowl.

Slice the apple thinly, then halve the slices and toss into the bowl.

Pour the vinaigrette onto the endives and apples and, with clean hands, gently massage it into the salad so it is well coated. Divide the salad onto four plates and garnish with the crispy lardons.

Saint-Tropez Crunchy Carrot Salad

SERVES 4

I spent a couple of summers living in Ramatuelle, a village outside of Saint-Tropez, and I would excitedly join the throngs of cars heading every Tuesday and Saturday to the famous outdoor market, marché de Saint-Tropez, *on* la place des Lices. *I would go early, park my car, and head to the harbor for a morning café to watch the superyachts wake up. Then I would weave my way back into the village to the market, which sold just about everything, including antiques.*

There was a vendor in the Saint-Tropez market that sold a carrot salad that I love. I would carry it, and a container of paella from another vendor, down to the beach for a picnic after my shopping was done. This recipe is the closest I could come to that carrot salad because his was made with new thin carrots, which gave the salad a flavor that is harder to achieve with older carrots out of season. Nonetheless, it is delicious.

3 tablespoons extra-virgin olive oil

2 tablespoons mayonnaise

1 tablespoon Dijon mustard

Grated zest from 1 organic lemon

1/4 cup freshly squeezed lemon juice

5 teaspoons sugar

1/2 teaspoon fine sea salt

1 pound carrots, scrubbed

3 tablespoons fresh flat-leaf parsley leaves, minced with kitchen scissors

In a large bowl, whisk the oil, mayonnaise, mustard, lemon zest, lemon juice, sugar, and fine sea salt until well blended.

Using a food processor or a box grater, shred the carrots. Add the carrots to the dressing in the bowl, along with the minced parsley, and mix thoroughly to coat and combine. Chill before serving.

Classic Bistro Green Salad

SERVES 4

When you are wishing for a simple green salad, the kind found in most French bistros, this is the recipe to use. The key, as always, is to use the freshest salad greens you can find, then serve with baguette slices and unsalted butter.

3 tablespoons white wine vinegar or red wine vinegar

1 teaspoon Dijon mustard

¼ teaspoon fine sea salt

½ cup extra-virgin olive oil

1 shallot, minced

8 cups Boston lettuce, or butter lettuce leaves, torn, or mesclun greens

½ bunch fresh chives, minced

In a small bowl, whisk the vinegar, mustard, and fine sea salt to blend. While whisking, slowly add the oil, whisking until the dressing is emulsified. Stir in the shallot.

Put the lettuce in a large bowl and pour half the dressing over the greens. With clean hands, gently massage the dressing into the greens so they are well coated. If needed, add more dressing and mix again.

Divide the salad among four plates, garnish with chives, and serve.

Red and Yellow Roasted Beet, Goat Cheese, and Walnut Salad

SERVES 4

This salad will turn you into a beet lover. You roast the beets, then slice them into a salad with apples, crunchy walnuts, and crumbled goat cheese tossed in a flavorful vinaigrette. If you like pickled beets, dice some and toss them into the salad as well. Use only the bulbs of the beets and save the beet greens to sauté the next day with olive oil and garlic for a vegetable side dish. And only use enough vinaigrette to just coat everything. If you have any leftover, serve it on the side for drizzling.

FOR THE SALAD

2 red beets, trimmed, scrubbed, and dried

2 yellow beets, trimmed, scrubbed, and dried

Extra-virgin olive oil, for drizzling

Sea salt

1 Honeycrisp or other sweet apple, peeled and thinly sliced

4 cups mesclun greens

$\frac{1}{2}$ cup chopped walnuts

4 ounces soft herbed goat cheese or French feta cheese

FOR THE VINAIGRETTE

3 tablespoons honey

3 tablespoons red wine vinegar

1 tablespoon Dijon mustard

$\frac{1}{4}$ teaspoon ground cinnamon

$\frac{1}{4}$ cup extra-virgin olive oil

Preheat the oven to 400 degrees F.

TO START THE SALAD: Place each beet on a piece of aluminum foil, drizzle with oil, and season with sea salt to taste. Wrap each beet in the foil, place on a baking sheet, and roast for 45 minutes to 1 hour, depending on the size of the beets, until tender. Remove from the oven, carefully remove the foil, and place the beets in a colander in the sink. When cool enough to handle, wearing rubber gloves, peel the beets. Put the beets in a bowl and set aside.

TO MAKE THE VINAIGRETTE: While the beets roast, in a large bowl, whisk the honey, vinegar, mustard, and cinnamon to combine. While whisking, slowly drizzle in the oil, whisking until well combined.

TO FINISH THE SALAD: Put the apple into the bowl with the vinaigrette and toss to coat. Thickly slice the beets, put them in the bowl, and gently stir to coat. Add the mesclun and toss to coat and combine. Divide the salad among four salad plates.

Garnish with the walnuts and crumble the goat cheese over the top to serve.

A Wreath You Can Eat

Around the holidays, I liven things up with a festive "wreath" created out of vegetables and lettuces presented on a big circular platter or carving board so people can reach in and pick out what they want to put on their plate. This works in the center of the table for a dinner party as well as on a buffet table. To fill out the green and red holiday theme, I scatter fresh pomegranate seeds over the greens and use cherry tomatoes to make an edible display that is a delight to the eyes.

Have you tried French feta? It's milder and creamier than Greek feta and most gourmet or cheese shops carry it. I whip it with ricotta, scoop it into a bowl, which I place in the center of the "wreath" for dipping, then arrange the salad elements around in a circle, using rosemary sprigs to finish the outer rim.

To the side, offer a plate of a thickly sliced sourdough, stacked high for drama next to a best-quality room-temperature French butter and a decanter of vinaigrette.

FOR THE VINAIGRETTE

1/3 cup white balsamic vinegar

4 garlic cloves, minced

1 tablespoon freshly squeezed lemon juice

1 tablespoon honey

1 tablespoon Dijon mustard

3/4 cup extra-virgin olive oil

1 tablespoon fresh basil leaves, minced

FOR THE DIP

8 ounces French feta cheese, chopped

1 cup whole milk ricotta, chilled

1 garlic clove, minced

1 tablespoon extra-virgin olive oil

1/8 teaspoon fine sea salt

TO MAKE THE VINAIGRETTE: In a medium bowl, whisk the vinegar, garlic, lemon juice, honey, and mustard until well blended. Slowly whisk in the oil until incorporated, then whisk in the basil.

TO MAKE THE DIP: In the bowl of a food processor, combine the feta, ricotta, garlic, oil, and fine sea salt and process until smooth and fluffy. Transfer to a serving bowl and set aside.

continued >>

FOR THE WREATH

8 ounces fresh arugula

4 large hard-boiled eggs, peeled and halved

2 pounds heirloom tomatoes, any color, quartered

4 radishes, thinly sliced

12 cherry tomatoes

1 thick slice watermelon, cubed

1 ripe avocado, diced

1 red onion, thinly sliced into rings

1 large cucumber

1 medium carrot

16 fresh basil leaves

½ cup fresh dill fronds, chopped

Pomegranate seeds, to garnish

Rosemary sprigs, to garnish

TO MAKE THE WREATH: Toss the arugula in a large bowl and drizzle with enough vinaigrette to coat thoroughly. Arrange the arugula salad in a large "wreath" (circle) on a serving platter or board.

Place the bowl of dip into the center of the wreath.

Decorate the wreath with the egg halves, quartered tomatoes, radish slices, cherry tomatoes, watermelon, avocado and red onion rings.

Run the cucumber over a mandoline, or use a vegetable peeler to get long thin, wide strips. Roll up the strips and arrange them over the salad. Repeat the process with the carrot.

Scatter the basil leaves, dill fronds, and pomegranate seeds all over the wreath and place the rosemary sprigs around its circumference.

To serve, place a large spoon to the side for the dip, along with a plate of thickly sliced sourdough, stacked as high as feasibly possible, and add salad tongs for people to serve themselves salad.

Potato Salad Piémontaise

SERVES 4

Potatoes, gherkins, tomatoes, ham, and hard-boiled eggs make up this hearty piémontaise French potato salad, a classic that can easily be a starter or a main course. It has so many flavors and textures going on, and is elevated in taste by the home-made mayonnaise. If you prefer not to consume raw egg, use 1 cup store-bought mayonnaise and mix in a little mustard and a squeeze of lemon juice. Also, try to dice all of the vegetables, ham, and eggs the same size.

FOR THE SALAD

2 pounds Yukon gold or russet potatoes, unpeeled

Sea salt

Freshly ground black pepper

4 firm tomatoes, coarsely chopped

1 (¹/₂-inch-thick) ham slice, cut into bite-size cubes

8 small gherkins, coarsely chopped

¹/₂ cup fresh flat-leaf parsley leaves, minced

4 large hard-boiled eggs, peeled and diced

Crusty French bread, for serving

Unsalted butter, at room temperature, for serving

FOR THE SAUCE

2 large egg yolks, at room temperature

1 tablespoon whole-grain mustard

1 tablespoon freshly squeezed lemon juice

³/₄ cup extra-virgin olive oil

2 tablespoons heavy (whipping) cream or crème fraîche

TO MAKE THE SALAD: Bring a large pot full of water to a boil over high heat. Carefully add the whole potatoes and cook them until tender but still firm enough not to fall apart. Drain and let cool so you can handle them, then peel, cut into small dice, and toss into a large bowl. Season the potatoes generously with sea salt and pepper.

Put the tomatoes in a colander in the sink, season liberally with sea salt, and let sit for 20 minutes.

Toss the ham into the bowl with the potatoes, along with the gherkins, parsley, and eggs.

Rinse the tomatoes, then pat dry with a paper towel and toss them into the bowl. Cover the bowl and refrigerate the salad while you make the sauce.

TO MAKE THE SAUCE: In a blender, combine the egg yolks, mustard, and lemon juice and blend for 30 seconds. With the machine running, add the oil in droplets, very slowly at first, then in a thin stream until a mayonnaise forms. Transfer to a medium bowl and whisk in the heavy cream. Pour the sauce over the potato salad and stir gently to coat and combine. Re-cover the bowl and refrigerate the salad until chilled well.

Serve with crusty bread and butter to the side.

My Favorite Spring Asparagus and Pea Salad

SERVES 4 TO 6

Everyone who knows me expects to be served this salad when they come to visit. It's my favorite spring salad that I love well chilled. It's full of flavor and crunch and capitalizes on in-season spring asparagus and peas. Try it and you will see what I mean.

FOR THE DRESSING

2 shallots, sliced

2 scallions, sliced

24 fresh basil leaves

3 flat-leaf parsley sprigs, leaves only

5 tablespoons extra-virgin olive oil, plus more as needed

Juice of 1 organic lemon

4 teaspoons red wine vinegar, plus more as needed

1 tablespoon mayonnaise

1 teaspoon Dijon mustard

$\frac{1}{2}$ teaspoon sea salt

FOR THE SALAD

12 small new potatoes or fingerlings

20 asparagus spears, woody ends trimmed, cut into $\frac{1}{2}$-inch pieces

1 tablespoon extra-virgin olive oil

$\frac{1}{4}$ teaspoon sea salt

2 cups frozen peas or fresh, if possible

1 red bell pepper, cut into $\frac{1}{2}$-inch pieces

1 cup fresh dill fonds, finely chopped

$\frac{1}{2}$ cup fresh mint leaves, finely chopped

TO MAKE THE DRESSING: In the bowl of a food processor, combine the shallots, scallions, basil, parsley, oil, lemon juice, vinegar, mayonnaise, mustard, and sea salt. Process until well blended. Taste and add more oil or vinegar, as needed.

TO MAKE THE SALAD: Bring a large pot of water to a boil over high heat. Carefully add the potatoes and cook until tender. Drain and transfer to a large bowl.

In a large nonstick skillet over medium-high heat, toss together the asparagus, oil, and sea salt and cook just until just barely tender. You want the asparagus still crisp. Throw in the peas and sauté until just cooked through. You want them still crisp, not mushy. Transfer the asparagus and peas to the bowl with the potatoes. Let the vegetables cool to room temperature.

Add the bell pepper. Pour in the dressing and gently toss to coat and combine. Scatter the dill and mint over the top, toss to mix thoroughly. Chill before serving.

Shredded Winter Vegetable Salad

The game changer for me when making some salads and soups is to rely on the shredding disk of my food processor to effortlessly shred hardy vegetables. This colorful, healthy salad comes together quickly using this technique.

FOR THE SALAD

12 Brussels sprouts, trimmed

8 radishes, trimmed

4 carrots

1 parsnip, peeled

½ head small red cabbage

1 bunch fresh chives

1 bunch fresh parsley, leaves only

FOR THE DRESSING

½ cup pimiento-stuffed green olives

⅔ cup extra-virgin olive oil

Grated zest of 1 organic orange

Juice of 1 organic orange

3 tablespoons white or white balsamic vinegar

2 tablespoons honey

2 garlic cloves, sliced

1 teaspoon Dijon mustard

TO MAKE THE SALAD: Using a food processor fitted with the shredding disk, shred the Brussels sprouts, then transfer them to a large bowl. Do the same with the radishes, carrots, and parsnip, adding each to the bowl after shredding.

Cut the cabbage into pieces that will fit into the feed tube, shred, and add to the bowl.

Unplug the food processor, remove the shredding disk, insert the steel blade, plug the food processor in, and with the machine running, toss in the chives and parsley to mince. Add the herbs to the salad bowl.

TO MAKE THE DRESSING: In the bowl of a food processor, combine the olives, oil, orange zest, orange juice, vinegar, honey, garlic, and mustard and process until smooth. Pour the dressing over the vegetables and toss well to coat and combine.

Camargue Rice Salad

The Camargue region in southwest France is one of the oldest rice-growing regions in Europe, famous for its red rice, which you can order online. Apparently, in the 1980s, the typical white rice grown in Camargue cross-pollinated with wild red rice to produce what we now know as Camargue red rice. The nutty flavor of this beautiful rice and its slight chewiness help create a substantial salad combined with all the fresh vegetables.

4 tomatoes, coarsely chopped

2 jarred roasted red bell peppers, diced

1 green bell pepper, diced

1 cucumber, peeled and diced

½ cup pitted black olives, sliced

½ cup pitted green olives, sliced

3 tablespoons capers in brine, drained

2 scallions, thinly sliced

¼ cup extra-virgin olive oil

3 tablespoons freshly squeezed lemon juice

3 tablespoons mayonnaise

1 tablespoon Dijon mustard

4 anchovy fillets in oil, minced

2 garlic cloves, pressed or minced

4 cups cooked Camargue red rice or rice of choice

2 (5-ounce) cans oil-packed tuna, drained

½ cup minced fresh flat-leaf parsley leaves

4 large romaine lettuce leaves

In a large bowl, gently stir together the tomatoes, roasted red peppers, green bell pepper, cucumber, black and green olives, capers, and scallions.

In a small bowl, whisk the oil, lemon juice, mayonnaise, mustard, anchovies, and garlic to combine. Pour the dressing over the salad and mix well to coat and combine.

Add the rice and mix again. Let rest for 30 minutes at room temperature.

Crumble the tuna over the salad, sprinkle with parsley, and serve on lettuce leaves.

Maison
Olivero
Ravel
Tél : 04 90 35 02 49

MARSEILLE

FISH

There is a great fish shop in Antibes where I learned how to pick out fish by watching the shoppers and listening to the instructions given to them by the owner. Obviously, the first most essential thing to note is smell. Fresh fish and shellfish have no smell. The second most essential thing to look for when buying fish is clear bright eyes. They should not be dull or dry or glazed over. The owner assured me that if I did those two things, smell the fish and look at the eyes, that I would be in good shape. So, I pass on his wisdom to you, so you can enjoy the bounty of the sea!

Sétoise-Style Sausage-Stuffed Mussels

SERVES 4

This is my favorite recipe in this cookbook to cook for dinner. It is absolutely delicious yet not well known outside of the town it is from in the South of France. This iconic dish from Sète, the largest and one of the most picturesque ports in southern France, is a surprising combination of mussels stuffed with sausage, cooked in a tomato and wine sauce, then served warm with rice.

Oysters and mussel beds are cultivated in the Thau Lagoon, hence Sète's love for mussels, of which they produce three thousand tons each year. You could call Sète the city of mussels.

FOR THE MUSSELS

3 cups loose sausage meat

1 ½ cups seasoned breadcrumbs

6 flat-leaf parsley sprigs, leaves only, minced

4 large garlic cloves, minced

1 teaspoon fine sea salt

2 large eggs, lightly beaten

24 large mussels

Cooked white rice, for serving

FOR THE SAUCE

2 tablespoons extra-virgin olive oil

1 small onion, minced

2 garlic cloves, minced

⅓ cup tomato paste

½ cup dry white wine, plus more as needed

1 medium firm tomato

TO MAKE THE MUSSELS: In a large bowl, combine the sausage, breadcrumbs, parsley, garlic, and fine sea salt. Using clean hands, mix everything until well blended. Add the eggs and mix again until well blended.

Scrub the mussels under running water, pulling off and discarding any beards. Discard any mussels that do not close when you tap them on the counter, or any that are damaged. Toss the mussels into a large bowl, cover with water, and let rest for 5 minutes, then swish the mussels in the water and drain to ensure any sand is discarded.

Place the mussels in a Dutch oven, with no liquid, over medium heat. Cover the pot and cook until they just open. Using a slotted spoon, immediately remove the mussels from the pot and let cool. Discard any mussels that have not opened. Pour their precious liquid from the Dutch oven into a small bowl (you should have about ½ cup), as it is the secret addition to the tomato sauce that yields such incredible flavor.

TO MAKE THE SAUCE: Place the Dutch oven over medium heat and pour in the oil to heat. Add the onion and cook until soft. Add the garlic and cook for 2 minutes. Add the tomato paste and cook, stirring, so the pastes dries out slightly. Pour in the wine and stir well. Cook for 1 minute. Using the large holes of a box grater, grate the tomato right into the sauce. Stir in the reserved mussel broth.

Fill each mussel with stuffing and close with the top half of the shell. Snuggle the mussels into the tomato sauce so they are almost covered; if there is not enough sauce to cover, add a bit more wine or water. Slip a heavy plate over the top of the mussels, place something heavy over the plate to weigh it down, then put the lid on the pot. Simmer gently over low heat for 30 minutes.

To serve, place rice in the center of each plate, then arrange 6 mussels in a wagon wheel formation around the rice. Spoon the sauce over the mussels.

Sea Scallop Brochette Persillade

Persillade is a mixture of fresh parsley and garlic, usually used as a condiment or sauce. And "brochette" means cooked on a skewer. When you put the two together, you can whip up almost anything on a grill or grill pan on the stove, and do it anywhere from your backyard to a beach to your kitchen, and turn out a delicious meal. This dish is made with large sea scallops threaded on skewers and served with the persillade sauce over rice. You will need four (8- to 10-inch) bamboo or metal skewers for the scallops.

FOR THE PERSILLADE SAUCE

1 cup tightly packed fresh flat-leaf parsley leaves

$\frac{1}{3}$ cup extra-virgin olive oil, plus more as needed

2 garlic cloves, minced

2 tablespoons freshly squeezed lemon juice

$\frac{1}{2}$ teaspoon fine sea salt

FOR THE SCALLOPS

2 tablespoons extra-virgin olive oil

16 large sea scallops, rinsed and patted very dry

Fine sea salt

Cooked rice, for serving

2 large organic lemons, quartered, divided

If you are using wooden skewers, soak them in water for 1 hour before cooking the scallops.

TO MAKE THE PERSILLADE SAUCE: In the bowl of a food processor, combine the parsley, oil, garlic, lemon juice, and fine sea salt and process until smooth. Add a bit more oil, if desired, to thin the sauce. Set aside.

Preheat the grill or a grill pan on the stovetop to medium-high heat.

TO MAKE THE SCALLOPS: Rub the oil all over the scallops, season with fine sea salt, and thread them onto skewers. Thread a lemon quarter onto each skewer as well. Place the skewers on the grill and cook for about 4 minutes, turning a couple of times, until cooked through and opaque.

Serve the scallops over rice. Divide the persillade sauce over half of the scallops and around the rice. Place the remaining lemon quarters to the side.

Seafood Paella Camarguaise

The Camargue region in southwest France is a short drive away from Spain so you will find paella in many of the restaurants and at stalls in open-air markets. If you want to be authentic, you can order Camargue rice online to make this recipe.

What makes this French dish different from Spanish paella is the nutty-flavored rice from Camargue, the less-dry preparation, and often a combination of chicken and shrimp. In my version, I use only seafood.

Extra-virgin olive oil, for cooking

1 medium yellow onion, minced

5 garlic cloves, minced

1 red bell pepper, diced

2 cups rice

4 cups bottled clam juice

1 cup white wine

1 tablespoon ground turmeric

1 tablespoon sweet paprika

1 teaspoon fine sea salt

24 mussels

24 littleneck clams

1 cup fresh peas or frozen and thawed

8 large or jumbo shrimp, peeled and deveined

2 tablespoons unsalted butter, cut into small cubes

4 flat-leaf parsley sprigs, leaves minced

2 organic lemons, quartered

In a large pan or skillet over medium-high heat, heat a swirl or two of oil. Add the onion and garlic and cook for 2 minutes. Add the bell pepper and cook for 2 minutes, stirring frequently.

Stir in the rice and cook for 2 minutes. Pour in the clam juice and wine and add the turmeric, paprika, and fine sea salt. Stir and bring to a boil. Reduce the heat to maintain a simmer, cover the pan, and cook for 25 minutes or until the rice is done.

Meanwhile, scrub the mussels and clams under running water, pulling off and discarding any beards from the mussels. Discard any that do not close when you tap them on the counter, or any that are damaged.

When the rice is cooked, place the mussels, clams, peas, and shrimp on top. Distribute the butter cubes over the paella, re-cover the pan, and cook for about 12 minutes, or until the mussels and clams are opened. Discard any that do not open.

To serve, sprinkle the parsley over the top and garnish with the lemon quarters.

Salmon in Parchment
with Capers and Lemon

SERVES 4

I learned this cooking technique from a friend and chef at a restaurant that popped up on the beach for one summer season in Juan-les-Pins. I volunteered to help her get started in the kitchen during the first couple of weeks when the restaurant opened, as the restaurant was only a half-hour drive from my house and I always wanted to see behind the scenes of these beach restaurants, how they cook for a crowd in such crowded quarters!

One night, I watched her cook fish quickly, oil-free, on the stove, steamed in parchment paper. To do it, you will need a medium saucepan with a lid, or a Dutch oven, and a couple large pieces of parchment paper. Don't use wax paper as wax melts, and parchment paper is coated with silicon, making it nonstick. Bring the dish to the table to unfold the paper and serve from for a very special main course.

2 medium tomatoes, unpeeled

4 spears broccolini, stalks peeled

½ organic lemon, thinly sliced

1 teaspoon sea salt, plus more to season the salmon

2 tablespoons freshly squeezed lemon juice

⅓ cup dry white wine

2 tablespoons capers in brine, drained

12 large fresh basil leaves, torn into small pieces

4 (4-ounce) salmon fillets

Freshly ground black pepper

Cooked white rice, for serving

Place a large piece of parchment paper over the top of a medium saucepan or Dutch oven. Using scissors, cut a circle that is 4 inches larger than the pot, so the parchment will be large enough to fold over the food, using the top of the pot as a guide. Fit the paper into the pot. Cut another piece like this one and fit it in the pot over the first piece.

Slice the tomatoes into eighths and toss into a large bowl. Toss in the broccolini, then the lemon slices. Add the sea salt, lemon juice, wine, capers, and basil. Using clean hands, toss everything to coat thoroughly, then pour it all into the parchment-lined pot. Reserve the bowl.

Season the salmon fillets with sea salt and pepper, then rub them in the bowl to coat with any leftover sauce. Place the fillets on top of the vegetables in the pot.

Bring the edges of the first piece of parchment together, then bring the ends of the second piece of parchment together over the top, folding to form a loose seal.

Place the lid on the pot and cook over medium-high heat for 7 minutes. Reduce the heat to medium and cook for 7 minutes or until the salmon is cooked to your preference and the vegetables are tender. You might see steam escaping while it cooks; that is fine.

Spoon the salmon, vegetables, and lovely sauce out of the pot onto each plate to serve, passing the cooked rice to the side.

Grilled Swordfish with Antiboise Sauce

SERVES 4

Named after the village of Antibes on the French Riviera, this sauce is a kind of French salsa. Chunky with olives, tomatoes, and capers, it pairs well with seafood, if not on top of a toasted baguette!

FOR THE ANTIBOISE SAUCE

4 ripe tomatoes

2 tablespoons thinely sliced scallion, white part only

1 tablespoon capers in brine, drained

1 shallot, minced

8 fresh basil leaves, thinly sliced

2 tablespoons minced fresh flat-leaf parsley leaves

5 large green pitted olives, sliced

5 pitted Kalamata olives, sliced

1/4 cup extra-virgin olive oil

2 tablespoons freshly squeezed lemon juice

4 anchovies, mashed

2 garlic cloves, minced

Fine sea salt

FOR THE SPINACH

2 tablespoons extra-virgin olive oil

4 garlic cloves, thinly sliced

1 pound fresh spinach leaves

1/4 teaspoon fine sea salt

FOR THE SWORDFISH

Vegetable oil, for cooking

4 (8-ounce) swordfish steaks, at room temperature

Sea salt

Freshly ground black pepper

TO MAKE THE ANTIBOISE SAUCE: Peel the tomatoes, halve, drain the juice, and remove the seeds. Coarsely chop and toss into a large bowl. Add the scallion, capers, shallot, basil, parsley, and the green and Kalamata olives.

In a small bowl, whisk the olive oil and lemon juice to blend. Whisk in the anchovies and garlic, then taste and add sea salt, as needed. Pour the dressing over the tomato mixture and stir to coat well.

TO MAKE THE SPINACH: In a skillet over medium-high heat, heat the olive oil and garlic just until the garlic begins to take on color. Add the spinach and give it a quick sauté, just until wilted. Turn off the heat, season with fine sea salt, and keep warm.

TO MAKE THE SWORDFISH: Brush the grill grates with vegetable oil. Preheat the grill to medium-high heat (375 to 450 degrees F).

Rub the swordfish steaks with vegetable oil, then season both sides generously with sea salt and pepper. When the grill is hot, place the steaks directly on the prepared grates and cook 4 to 5 minutes per side, or until the fish is opaque and an instant-read thermometer registers 145 degrees F.

Divide the spinach onto the center of each plate. Place a swordfish steak on top of the spinach. Using a slotted spoon, ladle the tomato mixture over the fish. The liquid left in the bowl can be drizzled around the fish on the plate.

Salmon on a Lush Bed of Leeks

SERVES 4

A recipe seen scrawled on chalkboards in the spring, it never fails to please dinner guests. Plus, it is almost effortless to prepare and get to the table. Use only the white and pale green parts of the leeks as the dark green part can be bitter. Save those bits for soup.

4 medium to large leeks

2 tablespoons extra-virgin olive oil, plus more for the baking dish

2 shallots, minced

1 teaspoon sea salt flakes, plus more as needed

2 teaspoons Dijon mustard

3 tablespoons dry white wine, plus 4 splashes

3 tablespoons plain Greek-style yogurt

4 (4-ounce) salmon fillets

Ground white pepper

1 organic lemon, quartered

Slice off the dark green part of the leeks (save for another use or compost) and use only the white and very light green parts. Trim off the root ends, then halve the leeks vertically. Rinse the leeks under running water to wash away any sand or dirt. Dry with paper towels, then slice the leeks very thinly.

In a skillet over medium-low heat, heat the oil. Add the leeks and shallots, cover the skillet, and cook for 15 to 20 minutes, stirring frequently, or until very tender, almost mushy. Stir in the sea salt flakes, mustard, 3 tablespoons of wine, and yogurt and cook for 5 minutes. Taste for seasoning.

Meanwhile, preheat the oven to 350 degrees F. Coat the bottom of a baking dish large enough to hold the salmon lightly with oil.

Spoon the leeks and shallots onto the bottom of the prepared baking dish. Place the fillets on top and season with sea salt flakes and white pepper to taste. Splash each fillet with a little wine, then cover the dish securely with aluminum foil. Bake for 15 minutes, or until the salmon is cooked through and flakes easily with a fork.

Divide the leeks onto the center of each of four plates, place a salmon fillet on top, and serve with a lemon quarter to the side.

Weeknight Halibut in Basil Cream with Cherry Tomatoes

SERVES 4

You'll want to make this tonight. The fragrant sauce, the burst of flavor from the cheery cherry tomatoes, and the lightness of the fish over rice comes together in minutes.

½ cup dry white wine

3 shallots, minced

⅔ cup heavy (whipping) cream

½ teaspoon sea salt flakes, plus more as needed

½ organic lemon, plus 1 large organic lemon, quartered

2 tablespoons unsalted butter

4 (6-ounce) halibut fillets

1 cup fresh basil leaves, minced

Cooked rice, for serving

12 cherry tomatoes, halved

In a saucepan over medium heat, heat the wine until it starts to form little bubbles around the edges. Add the shallots and cook, while bubbling, for 4 minutes. Stir in the heavy cream, bring to a rolling boil, reduce the heat to maintain a simmer, and cook for 4 minutes. Stir in the sea salt flakes. Squeeze in the juice of ½ lemon and whisk. Taste and add more salt, as needed, stir, and keep warm.

In a large skillet over medium heat, melt the butter. Add the fish fillets and cook until golden and cooked through.

Stir the basil into the warm sauce. Do not cook it. Left fresh and raw it will retain its color and flavor.

To serve, spoon rice onto four plates. Place a fish fillet to the side, then spoon the sauce over the top. Scatter the cherry tomato halves over the plate and serve with a lemon quarter.

Sole Meunière, Charred Lemons, and Tomato-Caper Beurre Blanc

SERVES 4

Always so simple to prepare yet so very delicious, sole meunière is a preparation that translates to the "miller's wife" because you dredge the fish in flour before cooking it. You can use any fish in this recipe, yet sole is classic.

1 cup chicken broth

1 cup white wine

½ shallot, minced

4 sole fillets, or flounder or fluke

1 cup whole milk (optional)

2 organic lemons, halved

1 cup all-purpose flour

Sea salt

Freshly ground black pepper

4 tablespoons unsalted butter, divided

1 tomato, halved, seeded, and finely chopped

1 tablespoon freshly squeezed lemon juice

2 tablespoons capers

½ cup fresh flat-leaf parsley leaves, minced, divided

To begin the beurre blanc, in a saucepan over medium-high heat, combine the broth, wine, and shallot. Bring to a boil over high heat, reduce the heat to medium-low, and let the liquid cook down by half. Set aside.

This step is optional, but if you would like to ensure that your fish does not have a "fishy" flavor, in a large bowl, combine the fish and milk. Let soak for 30 minutes before preparing. Drain.

Preheat the boiler.

To char the lemons, put them on a baking sheet, cut-side up. Broil for about 10 minutes, or until charred, watching carefully so they don't burn. Set aside.

To keep the fish warm as you cook it in batches, place a baking sheet in the oven and turn the temperature to 250 degrees F.

Put the flour into a large dish. Pat the fish really dry with paper towel. Season both sides of the fillets with sea salt and pepper, then dip both sides into the flour. Shake off any excess.

In a skillet over medium-high heat, add 2 tablespoons of butter to melt and let it heat until very hot. One at a time, cook the fillets until golden. Frequently tip the skillet and spoon the melted butter over the fish while cooking. Transfer the cooked fillet to the baking sheet in the oven. Add the charred lemons to the baking sheet to keep warm as well. Repeat with the remaining fillets.

To finish the beurre blanc, clean the skillet and place it over medium heat. Pour in the reduced wine and broth mixture. Whisk in the remaining 2 tablespoons butter until melted. Add 1 teaspoon of sea salt, the tomato, lemon juice, capers, and ¼ cup parsley and stir to mix. Taste for seasoning.

Serve the fillets with the beurre blanc sauce spooned over the top and scatter each fillet with the 1 tablespoon parsley. Add a charred lemon half to each plate.

Cozy Cod Casserole with Loads of Veggies, Parmentier-Style

SERVES 4 TO 6

Antoine-Augustin Parmentier is famous for convincing the French public that potatoes were safe and good to eat, which was probably a hard sell because, up to that point, potatoes were called "hog feed" and fed only to animals.

By the late 1700s, potatoes finally became accepted, and dishes named after Parmentier became popular. Even today, people remember and honor him by leaving potatoes, which they inscribe with merci pour les frites *(thank you for french fries), on his grave in Père Lachaise Cemetery in Paris.*

Although hachis Parmentier, *ground beef with a mashed potato topping, is ubiquitous across France, the preparation is also made with fish or vegetables. For this version, I poach cod in milk, then use the same milk to make the mashed potato topping. I also melt Boursin cheese into the mashed potatoes, a fun twist my neighbor in France taught me.*

Extra-virgin olive oil, for the baking dish

FOR THE FISH

2 cups whole milk

3 garlic cloves, minced

1 bay leaf

¼ teaspoon fine sea salt

2 pounds fresh cod

FOR THE POTATOES

2 pounds Yukon gold potatoes

1 (5.2-ounce) package garlic and fines herbs Boursin cheese

3 tablespoons unsalted butter, at room temperature

¼ teaspoon ground nutmeg

½ teaspoon fine sea salt

Coat an 8 x 10-inch or 9 × 13-inch baking dish generously with oil.

TO MAKE THE FISH: In a wide skillet over low heat, combine the milk, garlic, bay leaf, and fine sea salt and bring to a simmer. Put the fish in the milk and poach gently for 5 to 9 minutes, depending on the thickness of the fish, until cooked through. Using a slotted spoon, remove the fish from the milk and crumble it into big flakes in the prepared baking dish. Remove and discard the bay leaf from the milk; reserve the milk.

TO MAKE THE POTATOES: In a large saucepan, combine the whole, unpeeled potatoes with enough water to cover and bring to a boil over high heat. Reduce the heat to medium and cook for 25 to 30 minutes until tender. Drain and let the potatoes cool enough to handle. Peel and quarter the potatoes and place them in the bowl of a food processor. Slice the Boursin into the processor. Pour ⅓ cup of the hot milk that you cooked the fish in into the food processor and process until the potatoes are mashed and smooth. Add more milk, bit by bit, as needed. Add the butter, nutmeg, and fine sea salt and process until smooth.

Preheat the oven to 350 degrees F.

FOR THE VEGETABLES

2 tablespoons unsalted butter, plus 4 tablespoons (½ stick) unsalted butter, melted (optional)

1 celery stalk, finely chopped, plus leaves

1 medium carrot, finely chopped

1 medium white onion, finely chopped

1 small head savoy cabbage, thinly sliced

1 cup fresh or frozen peas

1 teaspoon coarse sea salt flakes

½ cup minced fresh flat-leaf parsley leaves

TO MAKE THE VEGETABLES: In a wide skillet over medium heat, melt 2 tablespoons of butter. Add the celery, carrot, and onion and sauté for 3 minutes. Add the cabbage and cook for 8 minutes. Stir in the peas. Scoop all of the vegetables over the fish in the baking dish and spread into an even layer with a spatula.

Scoop all of the mashed potatoes onto the vegetable layer and smooth the top. Brush the top with 4 tablespoons of melted butter (if using). Sprinkle with coarse sea salt flakes.

Bake for 25 minutes. Before serving, garnish the top with minced parsley.

Cod Bordelaise over Root Vegetable Purée

SERVES 4

A fish dish that is prepared à la bordelaise *is baked with a crispy crust. When in a hurry, the French grab a frozen version at the grocery store to heat up at home. I do, too. But if you make it from scratch, it is a completely different experience. Here, I use panko breadcrumbs over fresh cod that bakes on top of a layer of puréed root vegetables, creating a luscious layering of flavors and textures.*

FOR THE PURÉE

2 medium sweet potatoes, peeled and coarsely chopped

2 parsnips, peeled and coarsely chopped

2 medium carrots, coarsely chopped

2 cups whole milk or cream, divided

1 tablespoon sugar, plus more as needed

1 teaspoon fine sea salt, plus more as needed

FOR THE COD

2 tablespoons unsalted butter

3 shallots, minced

3 garlic cloves, minced

Juice of 1 organic lemon

3 tablespoons minced fresh flat-leaf parsley

1 teaspoon fine sea salt

1 tablespoon extra-virgin olive oil

1/4 cup panko breadcrumbs

4 (6-ounce) cod fillets, at room temperature

1/4 cup white wine

1 tablespoon minced fresh tarragon

TO MAKE THE PURÉE: Put the sweet potatoes, parsnips, and carrots into a large saucepan, cover with water, and bring to a boil over high heat. Reduce the heat to maintain a simmer and cook until very tender. Drain and transfer the vegetables to a food processor or blender. Add 1 cup of milk and process until smooth. With the machine running, stream in the remaining 1 cup of milk just until you reach a consistency of "mashed potatoes." Add the sugar and fine sea salt, process, then taste and adjust the seasoning, as needed. Transfer the mashed vegetables to the baking dish and smooth the top.

Preheat the oven to 350 degrees F.

TO MAKE THE COD: In a skillet over medium heat, melt the butter. Add the shallots and garlic and cook for 5 minutes. Stir in the lemon juice, parsley, fine sea salt, and oil. Add the breadcrumbs and stir to coat thoroughly.

Arrange the cod fillets on top of the vegetable purée. Sprinkle the wine and tarragon over each fillet, then top the fish with the breadcrumb mixture, pressing it down with a spatula to even it out. Bake for about 25 minutes until the fish is golden and flakes easily with a fork.

Halibut Quenelles with Carrot, Fennel, and Leek

MAKES 24 SMALL OR 8 LARGE QUENELLES

The kind of fish quenelles that first made me swoon were those I had in a restaurant near Lyon that were as light as air and napped with a rich, creamy sauce spiked with Cognac. I can still taste that dish. That Nantua sauce, over the quenelles, is an ancient recipe more than two centuries old, made with a mirepoix (diced onions, carrots, and celery), crayfish, lobster or shrimp shells, reduced fish stock, white wine, and cream and takes hours to shop for and cook. I found an easier way to make quenelles and can whip up this dish with a roasted vegetable base that sets off the cloudlike fish dumplings nestled on top. It seems healthier and lighter and it tastes divine. You can swap out the fish listed in the ingredients with the same quantity of raw shrimp, raw salmon, or raw chicken. If you are making smaller quenelles and feeding more than four, double the ingredients when making the vegetables.

FOR THE VEGETABLES

Unsalted butter, for the baking dish

1 fennel bulb

Extra-virgin olive oil, for drizzling

Sea salt

1 medium leek

1 medium carrot, peeled

1 cup chicken broth

½ teaspoon herbes de Provence

Preheat the oven to 375 degrees F.

TO MAKE THE VEGETABLES: Coat the bottom of a 9 × 9-inch baking dish generously with butter.

Cut off the top stalks from the fennel and save for another use. Mince the fronds and reserve for garnish. Peel off any worn outer pieces. Halve the fennel bulb vertically, then cut it into very thin slices and place them in the prepared baking dish. Drizzle with a little oil and a sprinkle of sea salt.

Slice off the dark green part of the leek (save for another use or compost) and use only the white and very light green parts. Trim off the root end, then halve the leek vertically. Rinse the leek under running water to wash away any sand or dirt. Pat dry with paper towels, then cut the leek very thinly with kitchen scissors over the fennel in the baking dish.

Holding the carrot over the baking dish, use a vegetable peeler to peel paper-thin pieces over the fennel. Pour in the broth and season with the herbes de Provence. Cover the baking dish with aluminum foil.

Bake for 20 minutes (about the same time needed to make the quenelles) until the vegetables are soft. Remove, but leave the foil on the dish to keep the vegetables warm.

continued >>

FOR THE QUENELLES

1 pound raw flounder, sole, or halibut, cut into chunks, chilled

1 large egg white, chilled

1 cup heavy (whipping) cream, chilled

2 tablespoons minced fresh dill, plus more to garnish

½ teaspoon sea salt

TO MAKE THE QUENELLES: Meanwhile, fill a Dutch oven or deep skillet about three-fourths full of water and bring to a boil over high heat, then reduce the heat to maintain a gentle simmer.

Put the fish in the bowl of a food processor and pulse 14 times, then process until the fish forms a paste and pulls away from the sides of the bowl. With the machine running, add the egg white and process for 20 seconds, or until the mixture is very smooth and fluffy. With the machine running, slowly drizzle in the heavy cream and process for 10 seconds. Use a rubber spatula to scrape down the sides and process again until blended. Add the dill and sea salt and process for 5 seconds to blend. Transfer the mixture to a large bowl and gently smooth the top.

To form the quenelles, I use a soup spoon, or a large serving spoon to make larger ones. You can also use an ice-cream scoop. Starting at the far edge of the bowl of fish mousse, dip the side of your spoon into the mousse, pull it across to your side of the bowl, then up the side of the bowl toward you. The spoon will curl the mousse toward you and form an oval football shape, which is your quenelle. It is pretty much the same as you would scoop ice cream with a spoon toward you. You can turn the quenelle over in your hand to smooth the other side before dropping it into the simmering water to cook for about 6 minutes. Don't overcook the quenelles, or they will become tough. Use a slotted spoon to transfer to a plate. Repeat with the remaining mousse.

To serve, remove the foil from the baking dish, divide the vegetables onto the center of each plate, place the quenelles on top, and garnish the quenelles with some of the broth from the baking dish, then with some of the reserved fennel fronds and some dill.

Flounder with Heavenly Beet Hollandaise

SERVES 4

Hollandaise is one of the French "mother" sauces designated by Marie-Antoine Câreme, but I don't imagine Câreme dreamt of a derivative of hollandaise made with purple beets! This light, absolutely heavenly luscious sauce works magic draped over fish. Prep the beets according to the recipe, then make the fish. Then use the beets to make the hollandaise at the last minute so it is very light and silky with a vibrant color.

FOR THE HOLLANDAISE

2 medium beets, stalks trimmed, quartered

3 large egg yolks, at room temperature

1 tablespoon freshly squeezed lemon juice

$\frac{1}{4}$ teaspoon sea salt

8 tablespoons (1 stick) unsalted butter, melted and still hot

FOR THE SPINACH

2 tablespoons extra-virgin olive oil

1 (10-ounce) bag fresh baby spinach, chopped

FOR THE FLOUNDER

4 (6-ounce) flounder fillets

6 tablespoons extra-virgin olive oil, divided

Sea salt

Freshly ground black pepper

Fresh dill fronds, to garnish

TO START THE HOLLANDAISE: Toss the beets into a saucepan, cover with water, bring to a boil over high heat, then reduce the heat to maintain a simmer and cook for 30 to 40 minutes until very tender. Reserve $\frac{1}{4}$ cup of the cooking water, then drain the beets. Wearing rubber gloves, peel the beets and set aside.

TO MAKE THE SPINACH: In a skillet over medium heat, heat the oil. Toss in the spinach and cook until just wilted. Set aside.

TO MAKE THE FLOUNDER: Rub the flounder generously with 2 table-spoons of oil, then season liberally all over with sea salt and pepper.

Place 2 skillets over medium heat, divide the remaining 4 tablespoons of oil evenly between them, and heat it until it shimmers. Place 2 fillets in each skillet and cook for about 3 minutes until golden underneath. With a wide spatula, turn the fillets and cook for 1 minute until they are opaque and cooked through. Turn off the heat and leave the fish in the skillets to keep warm.

TO FINISH THE HOLLANDAISE: In a blender, combine the egg yolks, lemon juice, and sea salt. Blend on high speed for 3 seconds until smooth. With the blender running, drop by drop, drizzle the hot melted butter into the blender, then drizzle it in a thin stream until the mixture comes together into a sauce. Add the beets and process until smooth. Add the reserved beet cooking water and process again until smooth.

TO SERVE: Divide the spinach onto the center of four plates. Place a fillet on top and ladle the beet hollandaise over the fish. Garnish each with dill fronds.

Pan-Seared Monkfish with Swiss Chard and Quick-Pickled Swiss Chard Stems

SERVES 4

Two days ahead of serving this dish, make the quick-pickled Swiss chard stems. Refrigerate the leaves, which you will use when you make the monkfish.

You hear most often that monkfish tastes like lobster, but I think its greatest attribute is that it is meaty and substantial, so served over the delicate Swiss chard leaves and made interesting with the surprising tartness of the colorful pickled Swiss chard stems, it becomes a dish to remember.

FOR THE PICKLED SWISS CHARD STEMS

1 bunch rainbow Swiss chard

1 small red onion

2 tablespoons minced fresh dill fronds

1 cup apple cider vinegar

¼ cup rice vinegar

¼ cup water

1 tablespoon sea salt

½ cup sugar

FOR THE SWISS CHARD

3 tablespoons unsalted butter

¼ teaspoon fine sea salt

Freshly ground black pepper

TO MAKE THE PICKLED SWISS CHARD STEMS: Cut the chard leaves off the chard stems. Wrap the leaves in paper towel and keep refrigerated until you make the monkfish in two days.

To make the quick pickle, cut the stems into 2-inch pieces. Thickly slice the red onion, then halve the onion rings into half-moons. Put the stems, onions, and dill fronds in a pint-size Mason jar with a screw-top lid.

In a small saucepan over medium heat, combine the apple cider and rice vinegars, water, sea salt, and sugar. Cook until the sea salt and sugar dissolve. Pour the hot liquid into the jar to cover the stems. Let sit for 30 minutes before securing the lid and refrigerating. The pickle will be ready to use in 2 days and will keep, refrigerated, for up to 2 weeks.

TO MAKE THE SWISS CHARD: When you are ready to prepare the recipe, coarsely chop the reserved chard leaves. In a skillet over medium heat, melt the butter. Add the chopped leaves, fine sea salt, and pepper to taste and sauté until the leaves are wilted. Remove from the heat.

FOR THE MONKFISH

4 (8-ounce) monkfish fillets

Sea salt

Freshly ground black pepper

3 tablespoons extra-virgin olive oil

1 tablespoon unsalted butter

3 garlic cloves, pressed or minced

Fresh dill fronds, to garnish

1 organic lemon, quartered

TO MAKE THE MONKFISH: Season the fillets on all sides with sea salt and pepper. In a skillet over high heat, heat the oil until very hot. Carefully add the monkfish. Cook, without moving the fish, for 3 minutes. Turn the fillets over, add the butter and garlic, and cook for 2 to 3 minutes, spooning the melted butter over the fillets while they cook. When they are just opaque, remove from the heat.

Divide the sautéed Swiss chard onto the center of four plates. Arrange some of the pickled stems over the leaves, top with a fillet, and garnish with a couple of pickled stems. Sprinkle some dill fronds over the top and place a lemon quarter to the side to serve.

POULTRY

The French honor chickens like no other country I know. They give them appellations, award them colorful ribbons to wear proudly, and rate them as to which taste best. Most would point to the *poulet de Bresse*, with its *appellation d'origine contrôlée* status, as the best chicken in France. I would point to the machine stationed outside grocery shops that has chickens turning around and around on spits, roasting. Below, at the bottom of the machine, there is a tray of cut potatoes and other vegetables that catch the chicken fat as the chickens turn. Those chickens are, for me, what chickens with ribbons are to true gourmets. I can't get enough of them and their delicious vegetables cooked below. The following recipes are some of the most popular ways to cook poultry. Bon appétit!

Autumn Harvest Chicken with Grapes, Apples, and Figs

SERVES 4

This is a simple chicken sauté, which means it is seasoned, cooked in butter until golden, moved to a plate while you deglaze the pan with a liquid, then the chicken is finished in the liquid. For this recipe, I coat the chicken in flour before cooking it. I use a Riesling wine from the Alsace region in northern France, and give it an autumnal garnish of apples and figs.

4 small apples

4 fresh figs, rinsed and dried

7 tablespoons water, divided

2 tablespoons unsalted butter

2 tablespoons all-purpose flour, plus more for the chicken

4 large bone-in, skin-on chicken thighs, or 8 medium or small thighs

Sea salt

Freshly ground black pepper

1 medium shallot, minced

1 cup white wine

1 cup chicken broth

2 tablespoons Calvados or apple brandy

3 tablespoons honey

2 cups seedless black or red grapes, rinsed and dried

Cooked rice or wide noodles, for serving

Preheat the oven to 350 degrees F.

Place the whole apples and whole figs into a baking pan. Pour 3 tablespoons of water around the fruits and cover the pan with aluminum foil. Bake for 15 to 20 minutes until just soft. If the apples need more time, remove the figs and set aside, then continue to bake the apples. Adjust the oven temperature to its lowest setting and leave the fruit in the oven to keep warm.

In a Dutch oven over medium-high heat, melt the butter.

Place some flour in a shallow dish. Season the chicken generously with sea salt and pepper, then dredge it in flour. When the butter is sizzling hot, place the thighs, skin-side down, into the Dutch oven and cook for about 5 minutes per side until golden brown. Transfer to an ovenproof pan or baking sheet and keep warm in the oven with the fruit.

In the same Dutch oven over medium heat, cook the shallot for 5 minutes. Pour in the wine, broth, and Calvados and run a wooden spoon over the bottom of the pot to deglaze it, scraping up any browned bits. Stir in the honey.

In a small bowl, whisk 2 tablespoons of flour with the remaining 4 tablespoons of water until smooth, then whisk this slurry into the sauce. Cook until slightly thickened.

Halve 1 cup of grapes and toss them into the Dutch oven. If you chose black grapes, they will add a lovely purple color to the sauce as they cook. Return the chicken to the pot, cover it, and simmer for 20 to 25 minutes until the chicken is cooked through and no longer pink.

To serve, place rice in the center of each plate, then divide the chicken and sauce among the plates. Garnish each plate with 1 baked apple, 1 baked fig, and the remaining grapes.

Basque Country Chicken with Multicolored Peppers

SERVES 4

A cheerful dish from the Basque country in southwest France, chicken piperade is cooked with red, green, and yellow peppers until they almost melt, plus shallots, tomatoes, and garlic. If you can find it, use smoked paprika, piment d'espelette, *from the mountain village of that name in the Basque country.*

6 tablespoons extra-virgin olive oil, divided

4 garlic cloves, thinly sliced

3 shallots, minced

2 red bell peppers, thinly sliced

1 orange or yellow bell pepper, thinly sliced

1 green bell pepper, thinly sliced

1 yellow onion, thinly sliced

3 tablespoons brandy

¾ cup dry white wine

1 chicken bouillon cube

2 pounds fresh plum tomatoes, coarsely chopped

½ teaspoon smoked paprika

1 teaspoon fine sea salt

2 teaspoons sugar

3 thyme sprigs, leaves only

1 (4-pound) whole chicken, cut up, or 8 drumsticks or 8 bone-in, skin-on thighs

Sea salt

Freshly ground black pepper

Cooked rice, for serving

¼ cup minced fresh flat-leaf parsley leaves

In a Dutch oven over low heat, heat 3 tablespoons of oil. Add the garlic, shallots, red, orange, and green bell peppers, and onion and cook for 30 minutes until the vegetables are very soft. Pour in the brandy and wine, then crumble in the bouillon cube. Stir. Increase the heat to medium and cook until the liquid is reduced by half.

Preheat the oven to 400 degrees F.

Add the tomatoes to the pot and cook for 20 minutes until everything is very soft. Add the paprika, fine sea salt, sugar, and thyme and stir to combine.

Season the chicken generously on all sides with sea salt and pepper.

In a large skillet over medium heat, heat the remaining 3 tablespoons of oil. Carefully add the chicken and cook, turning, until browned on all sides. Transfer the chicken to the Dutch oven, cover the pot, and place it in the oven. Bake for 20 minutes, or until the chicken is cooked through and no longer pink.

Serve the chicken, vegetables, and sauce over rice with a sprinkle of minced parsley.

Chicken Chasseur

SERVES 4

The French word "chasseur" means "hunter," so this dish was traditionally made with whatever wild game was hunted that day. As the story goes, on their walk home the hunters would gather wild herbs and mushrooms to use when cooking their game, so this dish has a sauce with loads of mushrooms and herbs, tailor-made for cooking in a Dutch oven. I don't cook off the brandy or Cognac because it mellows during cooking and I like the flavor it adds.

FOR THE CHICKEN

8 bone-in, skin-on chicken thighs

1 teaspoon fine sea salt

Freshly ground black pepper

3 tablespoons extra-virgin olive oil

Cooked rice, for serving

FOR THE SAUCE

2 large shallots, minced

3 large garlic cloves, finely chopped

8 ounces baby bella mushrooms, coarsely chopped

1 chicken bouillon cube

1 cup dry white wine

2 medium tomatoes, unpeeled, finely chopped

2 tablespoons tomato paste

1 tablespoon coarsely chopped fresh tarragon leaves

1 tablespoon fresh thyme leaves

2 teaspoons coarsely chopped fresh flat-leaf parsley leaves

¼ cup brandy or Cognac

8 ounces white mushrooms, stems halved, small caps left whole

1 tablespoon unsalted butter, at room temperature (optional)

1 tablespoon all-purpose flour (optional)

TO MAKE THE CHICKEN: Season the chicken generously with fine sea salt and pepper.

In a Dutch oven or large skillet over medium heat, heat the oil. Add the chicken to the pot, skin-side down, and cook for about 5 minutes until the skin is golden. Flip and cook for about 5 minutes on the other side. Transfer to a plate.

TO MAKE THE SAUCE: Turn the heat under the pot to medium-low, add the shallots and garlic, and cook for 3 minutes. Add the baby bella mushrooms and cook for 3 minutes.

Crumble in the bouillon cube, then pour in the wine and add the tomatoes, tomato paste, tarragon, thyme, parsley, and brandy. Bring to a simmer.

Snuggle the chicken thighs into the sauce and cover the pot. Simmer for 30 minutes. Add the white mushroom stems and caps, re-cover the pot, and simmer for 15 minutes, or until the chicken is tender and no longer pink.

Divide the chicken among four plates. I like the consistency the sauce reaches in this dish, but if you prefer it thicker, in a small bowl, mash together the butter and flour, add this mixture to the sauce, and cook, whisking, until the sauce thickens. Ladle the sauce and vegetables over the chicken and serve with cooked rice.

Chilled Chicken Basil Salad

SERVES 4

This pretty green salad, taking its color from all the fresh basil in the homemade mayonnaise sauce, can easily be a main course served with baguette slices and a glass of rosé. If you don't want to consume raw eggs, use 1 cup store-bought mayonnaise, then whip it with the rest of the ingredients except for the egg yolks and olive oil in a blender before mixing with the chicken.

1 ½ pounds boneless, skinless chicken breasts

3 large egg yolks

1 tablespoon Dijon mustard

1 ½ cups extra-virgin olive oil

1 teaspoon sea salt flakes

3 garlic cloves, peeled

Juice of 1 organic lemon

2 cups tightly packed fresh basil leaves, plus 8 leaves, minced

4 large attractive lettuce leaves

Put the chicken breasts in a large saucepan and add enough water to cover amply. Bring to a boil over high heat and cook the chicken in the boiling water for 2 minutes. Remove from the heat and let cool to room temperature in the water. Slice into the middle of a breast to make sure it is cooked through and no longer pink. If not, cook until no longer pink. Slice the cooked breasts into 1-inch chunks, toss into a bowl, cover, and refrigerate.

In the meantime, make the basil mayonnaise. In the bowl of a food processor, combine the egg yolks and mustard. Process for 30 seconds. With the machine running, drop by drop, drizzle in the oil, then drizzle it in a thin stream until the mixture thickens to a mayonnaise. Add the sea salt flakes, garlic, and lemon juice and pulse twice to combine. Add the whole basil leaves and process for 30 seconds.

Add the basil mayonnaise to the chicken in small amounts, and stir to coat, adding more, as needed. Cover the bowl and refrigerate for 2 hours. Refrigerate any remaining mayonnaise for another use, or pass to the side at the table.

To serve, place a lettuce leaf on each plate, divide the chilled chicken salad among the plates, and garnish with the minced basil. Or you can serve as pictured with a small-bite presentation for a main coarse or as an appetizer.

Baked Coq au Vin

SERVES 4

One day, I felt like coq au vin *(chicken braised in wine), but didn't want to make a stew. So, I deconstructed the dish and cooked the chicken in the oven while I made a wine sauce for it. I liked the chicken breasts crisped under the broiler and the sauce to the side, which resulted in this recipe.*

FOR THE CHICKEN

8 thick-cut bacon slices

4 boneless, skin-on chicken breasts, at room temperature

Sea salt

Freshly ground black pepper

2 tablespoons vegetable oil

3 tablespoons unsalted butter

Cooked wide noodles, for serving

FOR THE SAUCE

2 tablespoons extra-virgin olive oil

2 medium carrots, thinly sliced

1 medium yellow onion, thinly sliced

3 garlic cloves, minced

8 ounces mushrooms of choice, thickly sliced, small ones left whole

2 tablespoons tomato paste

2 cups red wine of choice

4 thyme sprigs, leaves only

4 oregano sprigs, leaves only

1 chicken bouillon cube

1 ½ tablespoons all-purpose flour

TO MAKE THE CHICKEN: In an ovenproof skillet over medium-high heat, cook the bacon until it is browned and crisp. Transfer to paper towels. Remove all but about 1 tablespoon of bacon fat from the skillet. Leave the skillet over the heat.

Preheat the oven to 425 degrees F.

Season both sides of the chicken breasts generously with sea salt and pepper.

Add the oil to the skillet with the bacon fat and heat until it shimmers. Carefully add the breasts, skin-side down, and let cook, undisturbed for 30 seconds. Turn the heat to medium. Let the chicken cook without moving it for about 4 minutes, or until the skin is crispy and brown. Turn over the chicken and add the butter to melt. Cook the chicken for about 2 minutes while continuously basting it with the melted butter. Turn over the chicken again and put the skillet in the oven. Bake for about 8 minutes, or until an instant-read thermometer registers 165 degrees F. The chicken breasts are done. Remove from the oven, put the breasts on a cutting board, and tent with aluminum foil.

TO MAKE THE SAUCE: While the chicken bakes, in a large deep skillet or saucepan over medium heat, heat the oil. Add the carrots, onion, garlic, and mushrooms and cook for 5 minutes. Stir in the tomato paste, then pour in the wine and stir well to combine. Add the thyme and oregano and crumble in the bouillon cube. Bring to a boil, then reduce the heat to maintain a simmer and cook for 10 minutes, or until the vegetables are just tender.

In a small bowl, whisk the flour with a little water until you have a liquid paste, then whisk this slurry into the sauce. Return the sauce to a boil and cook, whisking, until the sauce thickens a little.

Preheat the broiler.

Just before serving, place the chicken on a baking sheet and run it, very quickly, under the broiler, skin-side up, to warm the chicken and crisp the skin.

To serve, mound noodles in the center of shallow bowls or plates. Slice the chicken breasts and place the chicken on the noodles. Spoon the sauce and vegetables around the noodles.

My Village's
Roast Chicken with Oranges

SERVES 4

It's all about the oranges in my village and, indeed, along the Riviera. Bar-sur-Loup is called the "village of oranges" and my backyard had two orange trees that kept giving me fruit to make jam, orange wine that my neighbor's husband taught me how to make, and this chicken. You will marinate it overnight and cook it the next day. To produce a juicy roast chicken, baste it often and turn it at least once. I like to serve this with rice tossed in the drippings of the baking pan to echo the flavor of the chicken.

½ cup freshly squeezed orange juice

Grated zest of 1 organic orange plus 1 orange, quartered

3 tablespoons extra-virgin olive oil

3 tablespoons white wine

3 large garlic cloves, minced

2 tablespoons light brown sugar

1 (4- to 5-pound) whole roasting chicken

Sea salt flakes

In a bowl large enough to hold the chicken, whisk the orange juice, orange zest, oil, wine, garlic, brown sugar, and ½ teaspoon of sea salt to blend. Add the chicken and turn to coat thoroughly. Cover and refrigerate overnight. Turn the chicken over in the morning, and leave in the refrigerator until 1 hour before you roast it. The longer you marinate it, the better it will taste.

Preheat the oven to 400 degrees F.

Line a roasting pan with aluminum foil, place a rack in the pan, then place the chicken on it. Pour 2 tablespoons of marinade over the chicken, reserving the rest of the marinade. Stuff the chicken's cavity with the orange quarters. Season the chicken liberally with sea salt. Cover loosely with foil.

Roast the chicken for 30 minutes, then remove the foil. Baste the chicken with the reserved marinade and roast for 45 minutes to 1 hour, or until the internal temperature registers 165 degrees F, or until the juices run clear. Transfer the chicken to a platter and let rest for 10 minutes before serving.

Chicken with Vinegar Sauce, Lyon-Style

SERVES 4

In Lyon, this dish is cooked with vinegar. The acidity of the vinegar cooks off leaving a lovely sweet-and-sour sauce that the chicken simmers in. I am absolutely addicted to it. It's true, French sauces make the meal, especially in this case. Sometimes a bit of cream is added at the end, but I find it dilutes the flavor, so I opt out of that tradition and make mine without cream. I also often double the sauce because everyone seems to want more for dipping chunks of bread into. I serve it with mashed potatoes.

FOR THE CHICKEN

2 tablespoons extra-virgin olive oil

Sea salt

Freshly ground black pepper

8 bone-in, skin-on chicken thighs

Mashed potatoes, for serving

FOR THE SAUCE

2 tablespoons unsalted butter, divided

2 shallots, minced

6 large garlic cloves, pressed

5 tablespoons red wine vinegar or tarragon vinegar

2 tablespoons tomato paste

½ cup chicken stock

½ cup dry white wine

2 tablespoons fresh tarragon leaves, minced

4 medium tomatoes, peeled, seeded, and diced

2 tablespoons minced fresh flat-leaf parsley leaves

TO MAKE THE CHICKEN: In a Dutch oven or large skillet over medium-high heat, heat the oil. Season the chicken generously with sea salt and pepper, then put it in the pot, skin-side down. Cook until the skin is golden and crispy. Flip the chicken and cook until the second side is golden. Transfer to a plate and tent with aluminum foil to keep warm.

TO MAKE THE SAUCE: Turn the heat under the Dutch oven to medium and add the butter to melt. Add the shallots and garlic and cook for 3 minutes. Pour in the vinegar, turn the heat to high, and cook for about 40 seconds, stirring with a wooden spoon to deglaze the pan, scraping up any browned bits from the bottom, as the vinegar reduces a bit and cooks off its acidity.

Add the tomato paste and cook for 1 minute, stirring, then whisk in the stock and wine.

Reduce the heat to low, add the tarragon and chicken, cover the pot, and cook for 15 to 20 minutes, or until the chicken is cooked through and no longer pink. Toss in the tomatoes, re-cover the pot, and cook for 2 minutes to warm them.

Serve the chicken and sauce over mashed potatoes.

A Chicken in Every Pot

SERVES 4

How can boiled chicken be so satisfying? For me, poule au pot, *or chicken in a pot, is chicken soup taken to another level. Celery leaves, parsley, and dill float on the soup, which you serve in a shallow bowl surrounded by the vegetables you also cooked in the broth. The chicken makes its entrance in the center of the bowl, crowned with a few coarse sea salt flakes.*

Where did the recipe get its name? Allegedly, King Henry IV wanted all of his people to be able to have "a chicken in his pot every Sunday," no matter how poor they were. Somehow, this recipe came forward in popular French culture with that name. I couldn't agree with King Henry more.

FOR THE CHICKEN

2 leeks

1 (3- to 4-pound) whole chicken, rinsed and dried

Sea salt

3 bay leaves

4 thyme sprigs

8 large shallots

3 large garlic cloves, sliced

1 small onion, spiked with 5 whole cloves

4 carrots, cut into 2-inch pieces

2 celery stalks, cut into 2-inch pieces, chop the leaves for garnish

8 small potatoes

1 chicken bouillon cube

Cooked rice, for serving

FOR THE GARNISH

¼ cup minced fresh dill fronds

¼ cup minced fresh flat-leaf parsley leaves

Coarse sea salt flakes

TO MAKE THE CHICKEN: Slice off the dark green part of the leeks (save for another use or compost) and use only the white and very light green parts. Trim off the root ends, then halve the leeks vertically. Rinse the leeks under running water to wash away any sand or dirt. Cut the leeks into 2-inch pieces.

Put the chicken in a soup pot or Dutch oven. Add 2 teaspoons of sea salt, the bay leaves, and thyme. Fit the leeks, shallots, garlic, whole onion, carrots, celery, and potatoes around the chicken. Pour in enough water to just cover the chicken, crumble in the bouillon cube, and place the pot over medium heat. Bring to a boil over high heat. Reduce the heat to maintain a simmer, cover, and cook for 50 to 60 minutes until the chicken is cooked through and no longer pink.

Transfer the chicken to a cutting board and let rest for 10 minutes before cutting into serving pieces. Remove and discard the bay leaves and clove-spiked onion. Divide the chicken pieces among four shallow bowls. Remove the vegetables from the pot and distribute around the chicken in the bowls.

Taste the broth and season with sea salt, as needed. Ladle the broth around the chicken in the bowls.

TO MAKE THE GARNISH: Garnish each serving with the reserved celery leaves, dill, parsley, and a sprinkle of coarse sea salt flakes. Serve with a small bowl of rice to the side that you can pour the delicious broth into as you eat the soup. Sometimes, the rice is cooked in the broth with the chicken, but this way you have a choice.

A Rustic Chicken Fricassée

SERVES 4

When we think of a chicken dish that might be served in a bistro or on a grandmother's table, it's usually this dish. In its simplicity, it is pure nostalgia. A bit of juicy chicken, some wine thrown in, a splash of cream, mushrooms, and tarragon and you have the quintessential French meal.

FOR THE CHICKEN

8 bone-in, skin-on chicken thighs

Sea salt

Freshly ground black pepper

3 tablespoons unsalted butter

Mashed potatoes, for serving

FOR THE SAUCE

3 garlic cloves, minced

2 medium shallots, minced

1 teaspoon fresh thyme leaves

8 ounces white button mushrooms, halved

2 medium carrots, grated

1 small celery stalk, minced, including the leaves

2 tablespoons all-purpose flour

3/4 cup white wine

1 cup chicken stock

Sea salt

Freshly ground black pepper

1 tablespoon minced fresh tarragon leaves

1/2 cup crème fraîche or heavy cream

1 cup minced fresh flat-leaf parsley leaves

TO MAKE THE CHICKEN: Season the chicken liberally with sea salt and pepper.

In a Dutch oven over medium heat, melt the butter. When it is sizzling hot, add the chicken, skin-side down, and cook until golden brown underneath. Flip the chicken and cook for 2 minutes. Transfer to a plate.

TO MAKE THE SAUCE: To the Dutch oven, add the garlic, shallots, and thyme and stir. Add the mushrooms, carrots, and celery and cook for 1 minute. Toss the flour over the vegetables and stir to coat. Pour in the wine and stock, season with sea salt and pepper to taste, and add the tarragon. Using a wooden spoon, stir to deglaze the pot, scraping up any browned bits from the bottom. Cook the sauce, stirring, until it thickens. Settle the chicken into the sauce, cover the pot, and simmer for about 25 minutes, or until the chicken is cooked through and no longer pink. Transfer the chicken to a plate.

Stir in the crème fraîche. Divide the chicken and mashed potatoes among four plates, ladle over the sauce, then garnish with a sprinkle of parsley.

Lemon and Olive Chicken over Olive Oil Mashed Potatoes

SERVES 4

Provençal lemon and olive chicken in a wine sauce over mashed potatoes is my idea of a perfect rainy Sunday meal, a sunny, cheerful dish to serve with a crusty loaf and chilled rosé. Lemons, olives, and olive oil are all native to the South of France and work so well together, a harmonious combination taken to an even happier level when served over mashed potatoes.

FOR THE MASHED POTATOES

3 large Yukon gold or russet potatoes

¾ cup whole milk

3 tablespoons extra-virgin olive oil

2 garlic cloves, pressed or minced

1 teaspoon fine sea salt

Freshly ground black pepper

FOR THE CHICKEN

8 bone-in, skin-on chicken thighs, at room temperature

Sea salt

Freshly ground black pepper

All-purpose flour, for dredging

3 tablespoons extra-virgin olive oil

1 tablespoon minced shallot

5 garlic cloves, pressed or minced

½ cup white wine

½ cup chicken stock

Juice of 1 organic lemon

Grated zest of 1 organic lemon

1 small carrot, grated

1 cup pitted green olives

¼ cup minced fresh flat-leaf parsley leaves

TO MAKE THE MASHED POTATOES: Put the potatoes into a large saucepan, add enough water to cover, and bring to a boil over high heat. Reduce the heat to maintain a simmer and cook for 25 minutes, or until the potatoes are very tender. Drain and let cool to the touch. Peel the potatoes, cut them into cubes, and toss them back into the saucepan. Mash with a potato masher or ricer.

Add the milk and mix well. Place the pot over medium heat and cook for 1 minute, stirring. Add the oil, garlic, fine sea salt, and pepper to taste and mix very well. Keep warm until ready to plate.

TO MAKE THE CHICKEN: Season the chicken liberally with sea salt and pepper, then dust it with flour, shaking off any excess.

In a large skillet or Dutch oven over medium heat, heat the oil until it shimmers. Add the chicken, skin-side down, and cook for 4 to 5 minutes until the skin is golden. Flip the chicken and cook for 2 minutes. Transfer to a plate.

Toss the shallot and garlic into the Dutch oven over medium-high heat and cook for 2 minutes. Pour in the wine, stock, and lemon juice and add the lemon zest. Stir to deglaze the pot, scraping up any browned bits from the bottom. Snuggle the chicken back into the Dutch oven, cover the pot, and bring to a simmer. Cook for 10 minutes. Uncover the pot, add the carrot and olives and simmer for 10 to 15 minutes until the chicken is cooked through and no longer pink.

To serve, divide the mashed potatoes onto the center of four plates, place 2 chicken thighs on top, ladle the sauce over, and sprinkle with parsley.

Warm Duck and
Walnut Salade Landaise

SERVES 4

From the Landes area of southwest France, known for its walnuts and ducks, this composed salad is usually made with sliced duck, smoked duck, or duck confit.

Salade Landaise typically also includes duck gizzards and might include foie gras. A mixture of hot and cold, the salad starts with a bed of greens that is then layered with tomatoes, hard-boiled eggs, white asparagus from the region, bacon, ham, or pine nuts.

FOR THE DUCK

2 duck breasts

8 ounces thick-cut bacon, cut into large cubes

2 thick slices best quality white bread or brioche, crusts removed

Unsalted butter, for the croutons

FOR THE VINAIGRETTE AND SALAD

1 medium shallot, minced

1 teaspoon honey

2 teaspoons Dijon mustard

4 teaspoons white wine vinegar

6 tablespoons extra-virgin olive oil or walnut oil

6 cups salad greens

2 tomatoes, quartered

16 yellow or orange cherry tomatoes

8 ounces whole walnuts or pine nuts

4 slices mousse de foie gras (optional)

1 endive, leaves separated

2 tablespoons minced fresh chives

TO MAKE THE DUCK: With a sharp knife, make shallow diagonal cuts in the duck breast skin. Place the breasts in a cold skillet, then slowly increase the heat under the skillet, from low to medium-low to medium to medium-high, so that the fat has a chance to melt and create liquid fat in the bottom of the skillet. When all the fat has rendered, turn the heat to high and sear the duck until it is crispy, then turn the breasts to cook on the other side until just barely still pink inside. Transfer to a cutting board and let rest for 10 minutes, then thinly slice the breasts and set aside.

Keep the duck fat in the skillet over medium heat. Add the bacon to the skillet and cook in the fat until crispy. Using a slotted spoon, transfer to a paper towel.

Toast the bread, butter the slices, then cut each slice into croutons and set aside.

TO MAKE THE VINAIGRETTE AND SALAD: In a medium bowl, whisk the shallot, honey, mustard, vinegar, and oil to blend. Place the salad greens in a large bowl, pour the vinaigrette over them, and, with clean hands, massage the vinaigrette into the greens until very well coated. Mound the greens into the center of four plates.

Arrange the tomato quarters, cherry tomatoes, nuts, and bacon over the greens and finish with warm slices of duck. Add the mousse de foie gras (if using).

Tuck the endive leaves around the perimeter of the plate in a daisy pattern and add croutons to each salad. Sprinkle with the chives to serve.

Easy Whole Duck à l'Orange

SERVES 4

The day before you want to serve this, you will marinate the duck overnight, so plan ahead. You will also need a roasting pan with a rack.

For me, roasting a duck is as easy as roasting a chicken. In my village, we pair duck with orange because we have orange trees that grow the bigarade *orange, the traditional bitter orange used for duck à l'orange. I have a soft spot for the pairing of meat and fruit, and this spot found a home in my backyard.*

My sauce is pretty simple. After the duck comes out of the oven, to the juices in the bottom of the roasting pan, I add broth, fresh orange juice, orange marmalade, and spices. Oh, yes. I also add a little Grand Marnier and serve this over wide noodles with slices of the roast duck.

FOR THE MARINADE

Juice of 2 oranges

1 small jar bitter orange marmalade, divided

2 tablespoons Dijon mustard

2 garlic cloves, minced

1/2 cup balsamic vinegar or white wine vinegar

FOR THE DUCK

1 (5-pound) whole duck

Fine sea salt

Freshly ground black pepper

1 cup water

Cooked wide noodles, for serving

TO MAKE THE MARINADE: The day before serving, in a medium bowl, combine the orange juice, half of the jar of marmalade (reserve the rest for the sauce), the mustard, garlic, and vinegar. Whisk well to combine. Place the duck into a deep glass bowl or large zip-top bag big enough to hold it and pour in the marinade. Cover, or seal, and refrigerate overnight.

TO MAKE THE DUCK: The next day, when you are ready to cook, let the duck come to room temperature, then remove the duck from the marinade and pat it dry. Discard the marinade.

Preheat the oven to 400 degrees F.

Using a fork, pierce the skin all over the duck without getting down to the flesh. Using a small sharp knife, cut shallow slits all along the breasts and the legs, without getting down to the flesh. Season the duck generously with sea salt and pepper, then put it on a rack in a roasting pan, breast-side up. Pour the water into the bottom of the roasting pan.

Bake for 25 minutes. Turn the duck over and bake for 25 minutes. Turn the duck again and bake for 20 minutes, or until an instant-read thermometer registers 165 degrees F. Remove the pan from the oven and carefully transfer the duck to a cutting board. Tent with aluminum foil while you make the sauce.

continued >>

FOR THE SAUCE

Juice of 2 oranges

Grated zest of 1 organic orange plus 1 orange, thinly sliced

1 tablespoon red wine vinegar

1 tablespoon sugar

1 tablespoon honey

2 cups chicken broth

2 garlic cloves, minced

1 tablespoon cornstarch

3 tablespoons water

3 tablespoons Grand Marnier (optional)

2 clementines, peeled and segmented

2 tablespoons salted butter

TO MAKE THE SAUCE: Pour any liquid from the roasting pan into a sauce-pan or deep skillet over high heat, or use the roasting pan on your stovetop. Add the orange juice, orange zest, vinegar, sugar, honey, broth, garlic, and remaining half jar of marmalade and bring to a boil. Reduce the heat to maintain a simmer. In a small bowl, whisk the cornstarch and water to blend, then whisk this slurry into the sauce and cook, whisking, until the sauce thickens a little. Whisk in the Grand Marnier (if using) and cook, whisking, until the sauce thickens. Lay the orange slices and clementine segments in the sauce to warm. Before serving, whisk the butter into the sauce.

Slice the duck and serve it over the noodles with the fruit and sauce spooned on top.

Duck Breasts in Red Wine Sauce in Under 30 Minutes

SERVES 4

Under-30-minute meals make dinnertime so much easier! This has to be one of the fastest meals you can whip up and one of the tastiest because duck breasts take only minutes to cook, the sauce perhaps 10 minutes, and the two together rival any restaurant rendition.

2 duck breasts

Sea salt

Freshly ground black pepper

2 shallots, minced

2 teaspoons all-purpose flour

$\frac{1}{2}$ cup red wine of choice

1 cup chicken broth

1 tablespoon balsamic vinegar

2 teaspoons Dijon mustard

3 bay leaves

2 rosemary sprigs

3 tablespoons unsalted butter

Cooked buttered noodles, for serving

With a very sharp knife, score the duck breast skin in a crosshatch pattern without cutting into the flesh below. Season each side generously with sea salt and pepper. Place the breasts in a skillet on the stovetop, turn the heat to medium, and sear the skin for 7 to 9 minutes until browned and crispy. Flip the breasts, drain off most of the duck fat into a measuring cup, and cook the other side for about 4 minutes, or until an instant-read thermometer registers 130 degrees F. Transfer the duck to a cutting board and let rest for 5 minutes. Cut the duck into $\frac{1}{8}$-inch-thick slices and tent with aluminum foil to keep warm.

Pour any remaining duck fat in the skillet into the measuring cup. Measure 2 tablespoons of fat and put it back into the skillet to cook the sauce. Save the remaining duck fat to use as you would any fat.

Place the skillet over medium heat, add the shallots, and cook for 3 minutes. Sprinkle on the flour, stir to coat the shallots, and cook for 1 minute. Pour in the wine, broth, and vinegar and add the mustard, bay leaves, and rosemary. Bring to a boil and let boil until the liquid is reduced by half. Taste and season with sea salt and pepper, as needed. Fish out and discard the bay leaves and rosemary. Whisk in the butter.

Fan duck slices on each plate, then spoon the sauce over the top. Serve with buttered noodles.

Festive Christmas Roast Turkey with Chestnut Stuffing

SERVES 6 TO 8

Can't get to Paris for the holiday? Why not have a French-inspired feast at home instead? Referred to as dinde de Noël, *a roasted turkey at Christmas has been a tradition in France since the nineteenth century.*

The stuffing is quite special, normally incorporating chestnuts, sausage meat, and Cognac or brandy, or it could be stuffed with foie gras and apples or truffles. The amount of stuffing made should stuff any turkey up to twenty pounds with some left over to bake in a separate dish. Save room for the stuffing!

A beautiful festive bird, candlelight, and a decorated tree set the stage for ringing in the holidays! On fait la fête!

FOR THE STUFFING

12 cups good quality white bread cubes (1 inch)

8 tablespoons (1 stick) unsalted butter

4 shallots, minced

4 garlic cloves, minced

Turkey giblets (from the turkey), finely chopped

2 cups loose sausage meat

2 cups jarred cooked, peeled chestnuts, quartered

1 tablespoon fresh thyme leaves

1 tablespoon fresh rosemary leaves, finely chopped

1 teaspoon coarse sea salt flakes

Freshly ground black pepper

2 large eggs, at room temperature

1 1/2 cups chicken stock

1/2 cup Cognac or brandy

Extra-virgin olive oil, for the stuffing (optional)

Preheat the oven to 350 degrees F.

TO MAKE THE STUFFING: Spread the bread cubes on a baking sheet in a single layer. Bake for 20 minutes until golden and dry. Transfer the bread cubes to a large bowl.

In a large skillet over medium heat, melt the butter. Add the shallots and garlic and cook for 4 minutes. Add the giblets and sausage meat and cook until just turning brown. Transfer to the bowl.

Add the chestnuts, thyme, rosemary, coarse sea salt flakes, and pepper to taste to the bowl.

In a small bowl, whisk the eggs, then pour in the stock and Cognac. Whisk well, then pour the egg mixture over the stuffing and mix to coat and combine. If more moisture is needed, add some oil or water.

FOR THE TURKEY

1 (13- to 15-pound) whole turkey, at room temperature

Fine sea salt

Freshly ground black pepper

Extra-virgin olive oil, to coat the turkey

2 cups chicken stock

TO MAKE THE TURKEY: Season the turkey's cavity with fine sea salt and pepper. Stuff the turkey with the stuffing, taking care not to compact it in the cavity. Any leftover stuffing can be baked in a well-buttered baking dish.

Place the turkey in a roasting pan, rub the turkey all over with oil, season liberally with fine sea salt, and tent with aluminum foil. Pour the stock into the roasting pan.

Roast the turkey for 20 minutes per pound. For the last hour of cooking, remove the foil so the turkey browns. Remove and let rest for 30 minutes before carving to serve.

SYNDICAT des ELEVEURS
BOVINS du GARD

MEATS

The local *boucherie* in most villages is a neighborhood mainstay and a source for learning how to cook all kinds of meat. They sell house-made sausages. They will grind beef for you. They ask you how you are going to cook it. They might suggest a marinade recipe. They spend time with you. And they know their meat. The butcher, the baker, and the café are, possibly, the three most prized stops in town.

Normandy Pork Chops with Calvados and Apples

SERVES 4

Hard apple cider, cream, and apples are most commonly found in pork dishes made in Normandy, usually as a stew.

I love thickly cut bone-in pork chops, at least an inch thick, well seasoned, and seared in a cast-iron skillet to get a lovely brown exterior. I pair them here with a luscious apple compote and serve with a sauce you would find in Normandy, made with sweet apple cider, cream, and Calvados.

4 thick-cut bone-in pork chops

Whole milk, to cover

2 cups water

Juice of ½ organic lemon

5 Granny Smith apples

4 tablespoons unsalted butter, divided

Sea salt

2 tablespoons extra-virgin olive oil

¾ cup fresh apple cider

¼ cup heavy (whipping) cream

3 tablespoons Calvados or apple brandy, divided

Tenderize the pork chops by putting them in a large bowl and covering with milk. Refrigerate for 2 hours.

In another large bowl, stir together the water and lemon juice.

Working one at a time, peel the apples, slice them, then coarsely chop the slices and toss into the bowl of acidulated water to prevent them from browning.

In a large saucepan over medium heat, melt 2 tablespoons of butter. Drain the apples and add them to the saucepan. Season lightly with sea salt and cook until very soft. Set aside and keep warm.

Rinse the pork chops and pat very dry.

In a large skillet over medium heat, melt the remaining 2 tablespoons of butter with the oil. When the butter foams, put the pork chops in the skillet and cook for 5 minutes per side, or until no longer pink inside. Transfer to a plate and tent with aluminum foil.

Pour off most of the fat in the skillet, add the cider, and bring to a boil over high heat, scraping up any flavorful browned bits from the bottom of the pan. Reduce the heat to maintain a simmer. Whisk in the heavy cream. Taste and add sea salt, as needed. Whisk in 2 tablespoons of Calvados, taste, and add another 1 tablespoon, if desired.

Add the pork chops to the skillet to re-warm. Gently re-warm the apples.

Put 1 pork chop on each plate. Divide the warm apples over the top of the chops, then spoon the sauce over the apples to serve.

A Simple Braised Pork Loin with Plum Compote

SERVES 6 TO 8

The sauce from this dish is fabulous, and serving the pork slices with fresh plum compote is divine. I offer this with mashed potatoes and some sauce drizzled over them. You can make the compote ahead and either refrigerate it or keep warm until ready to use.

FOR THE COMPOTE

2 cups water

1/2 cup sugar

Juice of 1/2 organic lemon

6 fresh plums, halved and pitted

2 cinnamon sticks

10 whole cloves

FOR THE PORK

1 (4- to 5-pound) boneless pork loin

5 garlic cloves, thickly sliced

6 tablespoons fresh thyme leaves, divided

Sea salt

2 tablespoons unsalted butter

2 tablespoons extra-virgin olive oil

3 cups whole milk

4 carrots, sliced into 1/4-inch pieces

2 Granny Smith apples, peeled and cut into small dice

2 ripe plums, peeled and cut into small dice

1 celery stalk, sliced

1 potato, cut into small dice

1/2 cup chicken broth

Freshly ground black pepper

2 tablespoons cornstarch

Mashed potatoes, for serving

TO MAKE THE COMPOTE: Pour the water into a saucepan and bring it to a boil over high heat. Whisk in the sugar and lemon juice. Reduce the heat to maintain a simmer, slip in the plums, and add the cinnamon sticks and cloves. Simmer until soft. Using a slotted spoon, transfer the plums to a bowl, reserving any liquid to drizzle over the plums when serving. Remove and discard the cinnamon sticks and cloves. Refrigerate or keep warm until ready to use.

TO MAKE THE PORK: Rinse and dry the pork loin. Using a small sharp knife, make small slits all along the loin and stuff garlic slices into the slits, then stuff in 4 tablespoons of thyme over the garlic in the slits. Season the whole loin generously with sea salt.

In a Dutch oven over medium heat, melt the butter, add the oil, then turn the heat to medium-high. When the pot is hot, place the loin in it and brown on all sides. Pour in the milk, add 1 teaspoon of sea salt, bring to a boil, then reduce the heat to medium-low. Cover the pot and cook for 1 hour. Skim away any milk foam on the sides of the pot as it cooks and discard.

Add the carrots, apples, plums, celery, and potato. Re-cover the pot and cook for 45 minutes, then check the pork to see if it is done. When the meat is tender and a meat thermometer registers 170 degrees F, transfer the pork to a cutting board and let rest for 10 minutes.

While the pork rests, pour the chicken broth into the Dutch oven and bring to a boil over high heat. Reduce the heat to medium-low. Scrape the bottom of the pot to loosen any browned bits, then taste for seasoning, adding more sea salt and pepper to taste, as needed. Again, if there is any milky foam on the sides of the pot, skim it away and discard. Stir in the remaining 2 tablespoons of thyme and cook for 5 minutes. Carefully transfer everything in the pot to a blender and purée until smooth. Return the sauce to the pot.

Ladle 1 cup of sauce into a small bowl and whisk in the cornstarch. Return to the pot and whisk to blend. Bring the sauce to a low boil and cook, whisking, until it thickens.

Slice the pork loin and place on a serving platter. Spoon the sauce over the pork. Serve with mashed potatoes, passing the compote in a separate bowl.

Veal Blanquette in a Lemony Cream Sauce

SERVES 4

The favorite stew of Inspector Maigret in the detective novels of Georges Simenon, and one of France's most loved dishes, this mostly white veal dish must even be served on white rice.

This is my chance to indulge my love for white onions, adding lots of them and lots of mushrooms, either little white buttons or all varieties at once. It depends on what I find in the market. And garlic (it's white). I also twist the recipe a bit by adding small cauliflower florets and chunks of parsnip, all cut about the same size. Even the ground pepper should be white, not black. But I do, like most others, add big chunks of carrot for their flavor and pop of color.

2 ½ pounds boneless veal shoulder, cut into 2-inch chunks

4 cups water

8 peppercorns

4 whole cloves

3 garlic cloves, minced

3 thyme sprigs

2 bay leaves

4 large white onions, halved, divided

1 large leek

2 large carrots, cut into 1-inch pieces

2 celery stalks, cut into 1-inch pieces, plus the leaves, coarsely chopped

2 parsnips, peeled and cut into 1-pieces

8 ounces white button mushroom caps

4 tablespoons (½ stick) unsalted butter, at room temperature

¼ cup all-purpose flour

Place the veal in a Dutch oven over medium heat, cover with the water, and bring to a simmer. Add the peppercorns, cloves, garlic, thyme, bay leaves, and 1 onion. Simmer for 1 hour, skimming away and discarding any foam that forms while the veal cooks.

Meanwhile, slice off the dark green part of the leek (save for another use or compost) and use only the white part. Trim off the root end, then halve the leek vertically. Rinse the leek under running water to wash away any sand or dirt. Cut the leek into 1-inch pieces.

Add the remaining 3 onions, leek, carrots, celery, and parsnips to the pot and simmer for 30 minutes. Add the mushrooms and simmer for 10 minutes, or until the veal is tender.

Using a slotted spoon, lift the veal and vegetables out of the broth and transfer to large plates. Cover with aluminum foil. Fish out and discard the peppercorns, cloves, and bay leaves.

In a small bowl, using a fork, mash together the butter and flour. Ladle ½ cup of hot broth from the pot and, while whisking, slowly drizzle it into the butter mixture, whisking until smooth. Whisk this mixture into the broth in the Dutch oven. Cook over medium heat, whisking, until the sauce thickens. Simmer for 5 minutes. Whisk in the lemon juice, fine sea salt, pepper, and nutmeg.

3 tablespoons freshly squeezed
lemon juice

1 teaspoon fine sea salt

1/2 teaspoon ground white pepper

1/4 teaspoon freshly grated or
ground nutmeg

1 cup heavy (whipping) cream, at
room temperature

3 large egg yolks, beaten

Cooked white rice, for serving

1/4 cup minced fresh flat-leaf
parsley leaves

1 organic lemon, quartered

In a medium bowl, whisk the heavy cream and egg yolks to blend. Very slowly and while whisking, stream in some of the hot broth, then pour this mixture into the broth in the Dutch oven and cook over medium heat for 2 minutes, whisking.

Add the veal and vegetables and cook just until they are hot again.

Serve over white rice garnished with the minced parsley and lemon quarters.

Provençal Stuffed Tomatoes on Rice

SERVES 4

Aside from being economical, these delightful Provençal stuffed tomatoes are served on a bed of rice that they are cooked on so it is an easy all-in-one meal.

In Old Town Nice, miniature stuffed vegetables are sold as walk-about snacks, and in most of the Côte d'Azur and Provence they make more of a meal, like this recipe I learned from a friend's grandfather who lived near Saint-Rémy.

3 tablespoons extra-virgin olive oil, divided, plus more for the baking dish

8 medium tomatoes

1 teaspoon sea salt flakes, plus more for the tomatoes

12 ounces ground beef or lamb

1 medium yellow onion, minced

3 garlic cloves, minced or pressed

2 tablespoons Dijon mustard

Freshly ground black pepper

1 cup crushed saltine crackers or breadcrumbs

1 large egg

2 tablespoons whole milk

1 1/2 teaspoons dried thyme leaves

1 cup raw basmati rice, rinsed well

1 1/2 cups boiling water, divided

Preheat the oven to 375 degrees F. Coat an 8 × 10-inch baking dish generously with oil.

Cut a thin slice off the bottom of each tomato so they sit flat. Slice off the tops and reserve. Working over a bowl to reserve the flesh and juice, use a spoon to carve out the centers of the tomatoes. Sprinkle the inside of each tomato with the 1 teaspoon of sea salt flakes, then place them on a paper towel, upside-down, to drain. Use a fork to mash together the reserved tomato flesh and juice. Set aside.

In a large bowl, combine the ground beef, 1 tablespoon of oil, the onion, garlic, mustard, sea salt flakes, pepper to taste, crushed crackers, egg, milk, and thyme. Mix well with clean hands, then stuff each tomato cavity with the meat mixture. If there is any remaining, it makes a great burger or meatballs. Cover each stuffed tomato with a reserved tomato top.

Spread the rice evenly in the bottom of the prepared baking dish. Arrange the stuffed tomatoes over the rice. Pour 1 cup of boiling water over the rice and around the tomatoes. Bake for 30 minutes. Take the dish out of the oven, pour the remaining 1/2 cup of boiling water into the rice, then bake for 15 to 20 more minutes until the rice is tender.

Spoon the rice onto the center of each plate and snuggle 2 stuffed tomatoes on top.

Whisk the remaining 2 tablespoons of oil and a sprinkle of sea salt flakes into the reserved tomato flesh and juice, then drizzle this mixture in a circle around the rice on each plate to serve.

L'Hamburger with
Caramelized Onions on a Brioche Bun

Yes, the French love their hamburgers. In addition to McDonald's being everywhere, ubiquitous in the student quarter of most French cities, some restaurants even specialize in hamburgers. At Joe Burger in Paris, they serve many types of burgers, but the one I usually order is the Montagnard, a hamburger with caramelized onions, melted Raclette cheese, lettuce leaves, sliced tomato, and a creamy, dreamy sauce.

Here is my version—a dish that begs to be eaten outdoors. I use Munster cheese, which is a great melting cheese from the northern region of France, and I make an easy blender tartar sauce normally served with seafood but it's delicious on a burger, too. If you are having french fries with your burger, try dipping them into the tartar sauce. Amazing. It is called "sauce tartare" and originated in France. If you don't want to consume raw eggs, use 1 cup store-bought mayonnaise, then mix it with the rest of the ingredients except for the egg yolks and olive oil for the sauce.

FOR THE TARTAR SAUCE

3 large egg yolks, at room temperature

2 tablespoons freshly squeezed lemon juice

1 tablespoon apple cider vinegar

1 teaspoon Dijon mustard

1 ½ cups extra-virgin olive oil

¼ cup sweet pickle relish

FOR THE CARAMELIZED ONIONS

2 tablespoons unsalted butter

2 medium red onions, thinly sliced

½ teaspoon fine sea salt

1 teaspoon fresh thyme leaves

2 tablespoons light brown sugar

TO MAKE THE TARTAR SAUCE: Put the egg yolks in a blender and beat for 2 minutes. Add the lemon juice, vinegar, and mustard and blend for 30 seconds. With the machine running, add the oil very slowly, in droplets at first, then in a very thin stream until you have a mayonnaise. Transfer to a bowl, stir in the relish, cover, and refrigerate until ready to use.

TO MAKE THE CARAMELIZED ONIONS: In a skillet over medium-low heat, melt the butter. Add the onions and fine sea salt and stir to coat. Cook slowly for 20 to 30 minutes, stirring often, until the onions are golden and tender. Stir in the thyme and sugar and cook for 5 minutes, or until the onions are caramelized. Remove from the heat.

FOR THE HAMBURGERS

2 pounds ground chuck

2 tablespoons mayonnaise

½ teaspoon fine sea salt

Freshly ground black pepper

4 slices Munster cheese

4 brioche sandwich buns, split

4 lettuce leaves (use your favorite)

4 thick slices ripe tomato

TO MAKE THE HAMBURGERS: In a large bowl, combine the ground chuck, mayonnaise, fine sea salt, and pepper to taste and mix well. Adding mayonnaise to the burger mixture keeps it moist and juicy. Form the burger mixture into four patties, taking care not to compact them too much.

Preheat a grill to high heat, or preheat the broiler.

Place the burgers on the grill and cook to your desired doneness. Just before they are done, place a slice of cheese on top so it can melt a little.

To assemble, place the cheese-topped burger on a bottom bun. Layer on the caramelized onions, lettuce, tomato, and tartar sauce, then the bun top and serve.

Grilled Rib-Eye Steak
with Sauce Gribiche

Normally, sauce gribiche, made with hard-boiled eggs, cornichons, capers, and herbs, is served cold over potatoes or asparagus. I like to serve it at room temperature with steak and small boiled potatoes so I can spoon it over both. I had the unexpected combination one day at a café and never looked back.

FOR THE SAUCE GRIBICHE

4 large hard-boiled eggs, peeled and halved

1 tablespoon minced shallot

1 garlic clove, minced

2 teaspoons Dijon mustard

1 tablespoon white or white wine vinegar

1 cup extra-virgin olive oil

2 tablespoons cornichons (gherkins, not sweet pickles), minced

2 tablespoons capers in brine, drained and minced

1 tablespoon finely minced fresh tarragon leaves

1 tablespoon finely minced fresh flat-leaf parsley leaves

Sea salt

Freshly ground black pepper

TO MAKE THE SAUCE GRIBICHE: Scoop the egg yolks into the bowl of a food processor. Dice the whites and set aside.

Add the shallot, garlic, mustard, and vinegar to the processor. With the machine running, drop by drop, then in a thin stream, very slowly drizzle in the oil until it emulsifies into a mayonnaise. Transfer to a mixing bowl. Fold in the cornichons, capers, tarragon, parsley, and diced egg whites, then taste for seasoning and add sea salt or pepper, as needed.

FOR THE STEAKS

2 (2-inch-thick) rib-eye steaks, at room temperature

Extra-virgin olive oil, for the steaks

Sea salt flakes

Freshly ground black pepper

FOR SERVING

Small boiled potatoes

2 ripe medium tomatoes, thickly sliced

2 tablespoons minced fresh chives

TO MAKE THE STEAKS: Preheat a grill to high heat, or a cast-iron skillet on the stovetop over medium-high heat.

Rub the steaks on both sides generously with oil and season liberally with sea salt flakes and pepper. Place the steaks on the grill and cook for 3 to 4 minutes per side, until a meat thermometer reads 130 degrees F for medium-rare; 135 degrees F for medium; 145 degrees F for medium-well, or 155 degrees F for well done. Transfer to a cutting board and let rest for 5 minutes, then slice into 1 ½-inch-thick slices.

TO SERVE: Divide the steak slices among four plates, surround with the potatoes, ladle the sauce gribiche over the steak and potatoes, and add tomato slices to the side to garnish. Sprinkle all with minced chives.

Pan-Seared Rosemary Butter Steak over Caramelized Vegetables

SERVES 4

I bought a cast-iron skillet years ago just to make pan-seared steaks once I realized how good they are cooked this way. This recipe pan-sears steak with rosemary- and thyme-infused melted butter and is served with caramelized onions, mushrooms, and potatoes. You will need two skillets to cook the steaks, or cook them one at a time in one skillet and keep warm in the oven.

FOR THE STEAKS

4 (8-ounce) 1-inch-thick rib-eye steaks, at room temperature

2 tablespoons extra-virgin olive oil, plus more for the steaks

Sea salt flakes

Freshly ground black pepper

3 tablespoons unsalted butter

2 garlic cloves, thickly sliced

2 rosemary sprigs

2 thyme sprigs

FOR THE VEGETABLES

1 large onion, thinly sliced

8 ounces mushrooms, thickly sliced

8 fingerling potatoes, thinly sliced

1 tablespoon Dijon mustard

1 tablespoon sugar

½ teaspoon fine sea salt

Preheat the oven to 500 degrees F.

TO MAKE THE STEAKS: Rub the steaks all over with oil, then season the steaks heavily with sea salt, pressing it into the steaks with your fingers. Season both sides with pepper. Let rest for 30 minutes.

In a skillet over medium-high heat, heat the 2 tablespoons of oil until it is sizzling hot. Carefully place the steaks in the skillet and let cook for 30 seconds without moving them to sear. Turn the steaks over and cook for 3 minutes on the other side. Put the butter, garlic, rosemary, and thyme into the skillet to melt. Spoon the herb butter over the steaks several times before turning them over and cooking for 2 minutes more while spooning the sizzling butter continuously over the steaks as they cook to your preferred doneness (for medium-rare, 145 degrees F; for medium, 160 degrees F; for well-done, 165 degrees F). Transfer to a cutting board and let rest for 10 minutes before slicing. Keep the rosemary to garnish.

TO MAKE THE VEGETABLES: Place the skillet along with the butter in it over medium-high heat and toss in the onion, mushrooms, and potatoes. Cook until the vegetables start to take on some color and turn tender. Stir in the mustard, sugar, and fine sea salt and cook for 3 to 4 minutes until caramelized.

Spoon the caramelized vegetables onto each plate, lay the steak slices over the top, and garnish with the rosemary sprigs.

Beef on a String with Horseradish Sauce

SERVES 4

"Boeuf à la ficelle" translates literally to "beef on a string," a cooking method where you tie the beef filet with string at both ends and lower it into an aromatic vegetable-flavored beef broth—so the bottom of the filet does not touch the bottom of the pot—to poach briefly.

Because of the cooking technique, I prepare this dish when I have company who I know will find it interesting to wander into the kitchen and watch how it is done and, perhaps, help with the vegetables. Some people cook the vegetables separately, but I toss them into the broth to flavor it, then pull them out with a slotted spoon as they are done, one by one, and transfer to a plate before cooking the tenderloin, which cooks quickly.

I serve this with a horseradish sauce, sauce raifort, *a lot of crusty bread, cornichons, and a little pot of Dijon mustard.*

FOR THE BEEF

2 pounds center-cut beef filet

FOR THE BROTH

1 medium leek

5 cups beef stock

8 small potatoes, unpeeled

3 medium carrots, cut into 2-inch pieces

2 celery stalks, cut into 2-inch pieces

½ small head savoy cabbage, cored and quartered

4 garlic cloves, thinly sliced

2 bay leaves

2 whole cloves

2 teaspoons fine sea salt

Freshly ground black pepper

½ cup minced fresh flat-leaf parsley leaves, stems reserved for the broth

3 thyme sprigs, leaves only

TO START THE BEEF: Tie the beef all along its circumference lengthwise with kitchen string, snuggly enough to keep the beef together as it cooks. Then, tie another piece crosswise at each end, leaving the string long enough to reach up to the spoon or rolling pin that will be laid across the saucepan to suspend it in the hot broth.

TO MAKE THE BROTH: Slice off the dark green part of the leek (save for another use or compost) and use only the white and very light green parts. Trim off the root end, then halve the leek vertically. Rinse the leek under running water to wash away any sand or dirt. Slice the leek into 1-inch pieces.

Pour the stock into a saucepan (large enough to hold the length of beef) over high heat and add the potatoes, carrots, celery, leek, cabbage, garlic, bay leaves, cloves, fine sea salt, pepper to taste, parsley stems, and thyme. Bring to a boil. Reduce the heat to maintain a simmer and cook the vegetables for 8 to 15 minutes, depending on how thickly you cut them, until they are just tender. Using a slotted spoon, transfer the vegetables to a large plate, then fish out and discard the cloves, bay leaves, and parsley stems.

FOR THE HORSERADISH SAUCE

2 cups crème fraîche or sour cream

1 tablespoon bottled prepared
  horseradish

1 tablespoon Dijon mustard, plus
  more for serving

2 teaspoons freshly squeezed
  lemon juice or balsamic vinegar

1 teaspoon fine sea salt

French baguette slices, for serving

Gherkins, for serving

Coarse sea salt flakes

Freshly ground black pepper

TO FINISH THE BEEF: Tie the loose pieces of string at the ends of the beef around each end of a wooden spoon or a rolling pin. Lower the beef into the broth just far enough so it's covered but that the beef is not touching the bottom of the pot. If there is not enough liquid for the beef to be covered, add water until it is. Simmer gently for 10 to 12 minutes for medium-rare, or longer, if desired. If you are like me and like a filet on the rare side, cook for 8 to 10 minutes. Transfer the beef to a plate and tent with aluminum foil to keep warm. Let rest for 10 minutes before removing all the string and slicing into pieces to serve.

Meanwhile, return the broth to a simmer and drop in the vegetables to reheat.

TO MAKE THE HORSERADISH SAUCE: In a medium bowl, whisk the crème fraîche, horseradish, mustard, lemon juice, and fine sea salt to blend.

When ready to serve, place a piece of beef in the center of each of four shallow bowls. Arrange the vegetables around the beef, ladle the hot broth over the top, and sprinkle with the minced parsley. Serve with the horseradish sauce, Dijon mustard, baguette slices, gherkins, coarse sea salt, and freshly ground black pepper on the side.

Instant Pot Beef Bourguignon

SERVES 4

Winter nights call for a hearty stew, and now that I recently learned to be comfortable cooking in my Instant Pot, I can whip up this amazing beef Bourguignon in no time. I have been making it since I was in my twenties, but this method works just as well and gives me time to set the table, make the salad, and have a sip of that same Burgundy that I am cooking with.

3 tablespoons unsalted butter, divided

3 pounds beef chuck, cut into 2-inch cubes, patted dry

Sea salt

Freshly ground black pepper

3 tablespoons tomato paste

1 tablespoon Dijon mustard

1 tablespoon fresh thyme leaves

6 garlic cloves, chopped

2 ½ cups red wine (such as Burgundy, Pinot Noir, or Merlot)

½ cup water

1 chicken bouillon cube

1 pound whole baby bella mushrooms, halved

12 shallots

8 medium carrots, cut into ½-inch pieces

2 tablespoons cornstarch

Cooked buttered noodles, for serving

3 flat-leaf parsley sprigs, leaves minced, discard the stems

Select Sauté on your Instant Pot, then add 2 tablespoons of butter to melt.

Season the beef cubes generously with sea salt and pepper. Toss half of the beef into the pot and sear on all sides. Transfer to a plate and toss the rest of the beef cubes into the pot and sear on all sides. Turn off the Instant Pot.

In the pot, combine the remaining 1 tablespoon of butter, the tomato paste, mustard, thyme, and garlic and stir for 30 seconds. Pour in the wine and use a wooden spoon to scrape up the browned bits on the bottom of the pot. Pour in the water, crumble in the chicken cube, and add all of the beef.

Lock the lid in place, turn the knob to Seal, select High Pressure and set the cook time for 20 minutes. When the cook time ends, let the pressure release naturally for 10 minutes, then quick release the remaining pressure by carefully turning the knob to Vent. Once you no longer hear steam being released, carefully remove the lid.

Drop in the mushrooms, shallots, and carrots. Lock the lid in place, turn the knob to Seal, select High Pressure, and set the cook time for 5 minutes. When the cook time ends, let the pressure release naturally for 10 minutes, then quick release the remaining pressure by turning the knob to Vent. Once you no longer hear steam being released, carefully remove the lid. Select Cancel.

Ladle ½ cup of broth from the pot into a small bowl and whisk in the cornstarch, then pour this slurry into the pot and stir to blend. Select Sauté, and cook, stirring occasionally, until the sauce thickens.

Serve the beef bourguignon over buttered noodles and garnish with the parsley.

Flat Iron Steak with Vichy Sweet Carrots

SERVES 4

Vichy style is a French cooking technique using water, butter, and a little sugar to create a shiny glaze. Carrottes à la Vichy were so named because the technique originated in the spa town of Vichy, where they used the famous mineral water to cook the carrots. If you were to be true to the original recipe, you would use bottled Vichy mineral water rather than tap water.

Paired with flat iron steak, a budget-friendly cut that you can pan-fry, and taking only minutes to cook, the carrots and steak create a deliciously quick meal.

FOR THE CARROTS

2 pounds carrots

1 cup water, plus more as needed

4 tablespoons (½ stick) unsalted butter

1 teaspoon light brown sugar

2 teaspoons honey

Squeeze of fresh lemon juice

¼ cup minced fresh flat-leaf parsley leaves

2 tablespoons minced fresh chives

Coarse sea salt flakes

FOR THE STEAKS

4 tablespoons extra-virgin olive oil, divided

4 (8-ounce) flat iron steaks, or 2 pounds flat iron steak, cut into 4 pieces

Sea salt

TO MAKE THE CARROTS: Slice the carrots on a diagonal in ½-inch-thick slices and toss them into a skillet over medium heat. Add the water, butter, and brown sugar and bring to a simmer. Cover the skillet and cook until tender, adding a bit more water, as needed. Stir in the honey and cook for 1 minute. Sprinkle in the lemon juice and stir in the parsley and chives. Remove from the heat and keep warm.

TO MAKE THE STEAKS: You can cook the steaks on a charcoal or gas grill following the same timing as cooking them on the stovetop.

Heat two skillets with 2 tablespoons of oil in each over medium-high heat until the oil shimmers. Season the steaks liberally with sea salt and pepper, place them in the skillets, and cook for 4 minutes. Flip and cook for 3 to 4 minutes more until each side is golden brown and the internal temperature registers 135 to 140 degrees F (for medium). Transfer to a cutting board and let rest for 10 minutes before slicing.

Divide the steak slices among 4 plates. Divide the carrots among the plates and add a final sprinkle of coarse sea salt over the top.

Broiled Lamb Chops
with Warm Potato and Herb Salad

SERVES 4

The bright flavors of the herbs in this delicious warm French potato salad pair well with the robust flavor of the lamb. The hint of fresh mint in the salad is a nice surprise.

FOR THE LAMB CHOP DRESSING

1 garlic clove, pressed

2 tablespoons extra-virgin olive oil

½ teaspoon fine sea salt

Freshly ground black pepper

FOR THE POTATO SALAD

1 pound small new potatoes or fingerlings

3 tablespoons extra-virgin olive oil

1 teaspoon fine sea salt

1 teaspoon Dijon mustard

1 garlic clove, pressed or minced

1 tablespoon freshly squeezed lemon juice or red wine vinegar

2 teaspoons minced fresh rosemary leaves

2 tablespoons minced fresh flat-leaf parsley leaves

1 tablespoon minced fresh mint leaves

½ cup arugula, finely chopped

FOR THE LAMB CHOPS

8 lamb chops, at room temperature

Extra-virgin olive oil, for the lamb

Sea salt

Freshly ground black pepper

TO MAKE THE LAMB CHOP DRESSING: In a small bowl, whisk the garlic, oil, fine sea salt, and pepper to taste to combine. Set aside.

TO MAKE THE POTATO SALAD: Bring a large pot of water to a boil over high heat. Add the potatoes and cook for 15 minutes, or until they are fork-tender. Drain and return to the pot.

In a medium bowl, whisk the oil, fine sea salt, mustard, garlic, and lemon juice to combine. Stir in the rosemary, parsley, mint, and arugula and mix well. Pour the dressing over the warm potatoes and stir to coat. Tent with aluminum foil to keep warm.

TO MAKE THE LAMB CHOPS: Position an oven rack about 6 inches away from the heat source and preheat the broiler. Place a wire rack in a broiler pan, or use a baking sheet.

Rub the lamb chops all over with oil and season liberally with sea salt and pepper. Place the lamb on the rack and broil for 5 to 6 minutes per side. Transfer to a plate or cutting board and let rest for 3 minutes.

Brush the chops on both sides with the dressing, then serve 2 chops per serving with the warm potato salad to the side.

Butterflied Leg of Lamb
with Stuffed Artichokes

SERVES 6 TO 8

Around Easter, tendrils of fragrant smoke curl upward from many villages. In ours, it usually carried the scent of spring lamb, which was being cooked either on an outdoor grill, inside on the stove, or in the oven studded with rosemary and garlic for le gigot d'agneau Pascal.

Since the flavors of lamb and artichokes go so well together, I am giving you recipes for both, for a full dinner that, perhaps, only needs a simple green salad on the side. Start a day ahead to marinate the lamb overnight, which makes it flavorful and tender. You can prepare the artichokes ahead of the lamb, keep them warm and, if desired, pop them back into the oven to warm again to serve when the lamb is ready.

Ask the butcher to make a butterflied leg of lamb for you, which is just a leg of lamb with the bone removed so the meat lies flat. I recommend cooking this on a charcoal grill for maximum flavor, but if you do not have one, simply cook on a gas grill.

FOR THE MARINADE AND LAMB

½ cup extra-virgin olive oil

½ cup freshly squeezed lemon juice or red wine

1 tablespoon fresh oregano leaves

1 tablespoon fresh rosemary leaves, coarsely cut

3 large garlic cloves, pressed or minced

2 teaspoons fine sea salt

1 (3 ½- to 4-pound) butterflied leg of lamb

TO MAKE THE MARINADE: In a very large zip-top bag, combine the oil, lemon juice, oregano, rosemary, garlic, fine sea salt, and lamb. Seal the bag, then massage the marinade all over the lamb. Refrigerate overnight, or for 24 hours. Remove from the refrigerator 2 hours before cooking.

TO MAKE THE ARTICHOKES: The next day, cook the artichokes ahead of the lamb. Fill a large bowl with water and add half the lemon juice. Pull off the outer leaves of the artichokes all the way around until you see pale green leaves, then stop. Cut off the stem, leaving 1 inch at the base. With a small sharp knife, trim away any small leaves at the base and the tough skin on the stem. Slice about 1 inch off the top of each artichoke. Use the knife or a grapefruit spoon to scoop out the choke at the center. Toss each artichoke into the bowl of lemon water.

Preheat the oven to 375 degrees F. Coat a baking dish large enough to hold all the artichokes generously with oil.

Pour the 1 cup of water into a large deep skillet or saucepan over medium heat. Fit the artichokes, open-side up, into the skillet, cover, and cook for 20 minutes. Transfer the artichokes to the prepared baking dish. Into each artichoke cavity, put 1 tablespoon of goat cheese.

Empty any water left in the skillet and return it to medium heat. Pour in the oil to heat. Add the breadcrumbs, herbes de Provence, garlic, fine sea salt, and remaining lemon juice, stir, and cook for 1 minute. Stuff the bread-crumb mixture into each artichoke. Sprinkle the Parmesan on top. Bake for 15 to 20 minutes. Remove from the oven and keep warm.

continued >>

158 | MEATS

FOR THE ARTICHOKES

Juice of 1 organic lemon

4 artichokes

3 tablespoons extra-virgin olive oil, plus more for the baking dish

1 cup water

4 tablespoons soft goat cheese

2 cups seasoned breadcrumbs

4 teaspoons herbes de Provence

2 garlic cloves, pressed or minced

½ teaspoon fine sea salt

1 cup freshly grated Parmesan cheese

TO MAKE THE LAMB: Preheat a charcoal or gas grill to medium-high heat, or position an oven rack 6 inches from the heat source and preheat the broiler.

If you are cooking the lamb on the grill, remove the lamb from the marinade and place the lamb on the grill, fat-side down. Grill for 11 minutes with the lid up. Turn the lamb over and cook for about 10 minutes, with the lid closed, then check that the internal temperature is at least 135 degrees F for rare or 145 degrees F for just pink.

If you are cooking the lamb under the broiler, remove the lamb from the marinade and place it on a broiler tray, fat-side up. Broil (6 inches away from the broiler element) for 15 minutes. Turn the lamb over and broil for 10 minutes, then check that the internal temperature is at least 135 degrees F for rare or 145 degrees F for just pink.

Remove the lamb from the grill and tent with aluminum foil. Let rest for 10 to 15 minutes before slicing.

Serve lamb slices with a stuffed artichoke on each plate.

VEGETABLES

Vegetables are their own star in France, rarely served on the same plate as the main course, but rather in their own serving plate or casserole.

If you go to any farmers market, it is vegetables that are the main attraction. The sheer variety, the fact that all the stalls are competing to offer the very best compared to the others, the celebration of the season, the rainbow of colors, everything about it excites me. I listen avidly to the advice of the farmers as to how best prepare their precious offerings and that's usually how my daily meals evolve, from the ideas I pick up at the markets.

The following recipes celebrate some of the most loved vegetable dishes in France.

Quick Artichokes à la Barigoule

SERVES 4

A specialty from the South of France, artichokes à la barigoule are made in spring with young artichokes that are braised with white wine and lots of vegetables. I love artichokes any time of year and, at a whim, sometimes when I don't have much time to cook. At those times, I use canned artichoke hearts, which I prepare with as many vegetables as I can find in the market that go well with them. This is the quick, or quicker, recipe I use. The artichokes pair well with fish or over pasta with an extra splash of good olive oil and a grating of Parmesan cheese. They're equally delicious cold the next day.

2 (14-ounce) cans artichoke hearts, drained

3 tablespoons extra-virgin olive oil

4 garlic cloves, thinly sliced

1 shallot, minced

1 medium carrot, halved lengthwise, then thinly sliced into half-moons

½ medium onion, thinly sliced

¾ teaspoon sea salt flakes

8 ounces mushrooms, any variety, finely chopped

½ cup dry white wine

½ cup chicken broth or vegetable broth

¼ cup minced fresh tarragon leaves

¼ cup minced fresh flat-leaf parsley leaves

Gently pat the artichokes dry with paper towels. If you wish, halve them vertically.

In a large skillet or saucepan over medium heat, heat the oil. Toss in the garlic, shallot, carrot, onion, and sea salt flakes. Cook until the onion and shallot are translucent. Add the mushrooms and cook just until they cook down.

Add the artichokes, wine, and broth and bring to a boil. Reduce the heat to maintain a simmer and cook for 6 minutes. Stir in the tarragon. Transfer to a serving bowl, or serve individually on plates, and sprinkle with the minced parsley.

Classic French Green Beans
with Shallots and Almonds

SERVES 4

Every New Year's Eve my father would make a roast with green beans and almonds and would serve the beans in a silver serving dish, where they took on a rather elegant demeanor. They looked pretty but were out of season and taste much better when you prepare them in spring when you can get fresh, tender farmstand green beans. This is a classic French preparation that can hold its own at either a chic dinner party or a casual lunch.

2 tablespoons fine sea salt, plus
   ½ teaspoon

1 pound fresh green beans,
   trimmed

4 tablespoons extra-virgin olive oil

1 medium shallot, minced

1 garlic clove, minced

1 cup sliced almonds

Bring a large pot full of water to a boil over high heat. Add 2 tablespoons of fine sea salt, then drop in the green beans. Cook for 3 to 5 minutes until just tender. Drain in a colander and run the beans under very cold water to stop them from cooking.

In a large bowl, whisk the oil, shallot, garlic, and remaining ½ teaspoon of fine sea salt until well combined. Toss in the hot beans and stir to coat well. Add the almonds and mix again, then serve.

Turnips, Parsnips, and Carrots in Mornay Sauce

SERVES 6 TO 8

French cuisine is known for its creamy sauces and Mornay is one of my favorites, a béchamel sauce with melting grated cheese, usually Gruyère or Emmental. Here, I make it with root vegetables and lots of cheese for a wonderful vegetable casserole.

FOR THE VEGETABLES

5 medium turnips, peeled

3 medium parsnips, peeled

2 medium carrots

FOR THE MORNAY SAUCE

3 tablespoons unsalted butter, plus more for the baking dish

5 tablespoons all-purpose flour

3 cups whole milk, at room temperature

Fine sea salt

$1/4$ teaspoon ground nutmeg

$1/8$ teaspoon cayenne pepper

$1/8$ teaspoon ground cloves

2 tablespoons Dijon or whole-grain mustard

$1 1/2$ cups grated Gruyère or Emmental cheese, divided

Dash paprika

TO MAKE THE VEGETABLES: Slice the turnips, parsnips, and carrots as thinly as you can or use a food processor fitted with the slicing blade.

Bring a large pot full of water to a boil over high heat. Toss in the carrots, reduce the heat to maintain a simmer, and cook for 6 minutes. Add the turnips and parsnips and cook until tender. Cook time will vary depending upon how thinly or thickly you slice the vegetables. Drain and pat dry.

TO MAKE THE MORNAY SAUCE: Coat an 8 × 10-inch baking dish generously with butter.

In a saucepan over medium heat, melt the butter. Whisk in the flour until coated and cook, whisking, for 2 minutes. While whisking, slowly pour in the milk. Cook the sauce until it thickens and is smooth. Whisk in 1 teaspoon of fine sea salt, the nutmeg, cayenne, cloves, mustard, and $1/2$ cup of cheese until the cheese is melted and the sauce is smooth.

Layer half of the vegetables into the prepared baking dish. Ladle half of the sauce over them. Layer the rest of the vegetables on top, then ladle over the rest of the sauce. Distribute the remaining 1 cup of cheese over the top, sprinkle with a little paprika and fine sea salt and bake for 25 minutes until golden brown and bubbling.

Asparagus with Blood Orange Maltaise Sauce

SERVES 4

Maltaise sauce is not as well-known as its mother sauce, hollandaise. It starts as a hollandaise that is then flavored with lovely sweet-sour blood oranges. If you can't find blood oranges, use Cara Cara oranges for their color, or any juicing orange because it is a sauce worth adding to your repertoire. It's quick to whip up in a blender and goes well with almost any vegetable or fish dish, even eggs Benedict!

2 pounds asparagus, woody ends trimmed

½ cup extra-virgin olive oil

FOR THE MALTAISE SAUCE

½ cup freshly squeezed blood orange juice, or any fresh orange juice

8 tablespoons (1 stick) unsalted butter

4 large egg yolks, at room temperature

1 tablespoon freshly squeezed lemon juice

¼ teaspoon sea salt flakes

Finely grated zest of 1 blood orange, divided

1 teaspoon sugar

8 thin slices blood orange, no peel, chopped

Wash and dry the asparagus. Place the asparagus in a large skillet, in a single layer (you may have to work in batches), and cover with water. Bring to a simmer over medium heat and cook until the asparagus is just tender. Using tongs, transfer the asparagus to a plate. Repeat with any remaining asparagus. Loosely tent the asparagus with aluminum foil while you make the sauce.

TO MAKE THE SAUCE: In a small saucepan over high heat, gently boil the orange juice until it is reduced to ¼ cup to intensify the flavor. Remove from the heat.

In another small saucepan over medium heat, melt the butter until it is very hot and bubbling.

In a blender, combine the egg yolks, lemon juice, and sea salt flakes. Blend the yolk mixture for 4 seconds, then, with the machine running, drop by drop, pour in the hot melted butter in a very thin stream and process for 40 seconds, or until thickened. (The lemon juice and hot butter will "cook" the egg yolks).

Pour in the reduced blood orange juice, add half the orange zest and sugar, and process until blended. Transfer to a bowl and stir in the orange pieces.

To serve, divide the asparagus among four plates and drizzle the sauce over the top, saving most of the sauce to be offered in a small bowl to the side. Sprinkle the remaining zest over the asparagus.

Warm Leeks in Vinaigrette

SERVES 4

Equally good warm or chilled, or the next day, these dressed leeks with the added crunch of finely chopped walnuts and the briny saltiness of capers make a lovely dish all on its own. Serve it with a stack of sliced rustic farmhouse bread and a great French butter on the side.

8 medium leeks

2 garlic cloves, pressed or minced

$1/2$ cup extra-virgin olive oil

2 tablespoons Dijon mustard

2 tablespoons white or white wine vinegar

$1/4$ teaspoon fine sea salt

1 tablespoon minced shallot

$1/3$ cup finely chopped walnuts

1 tablespoon capers in brine, drained (optional)

Slice off the dark green part of the leeks (save for another use or compost) and use only the white and very light green parts. Trim off the root ends, then halve the leeks vertically. Rinse the leeks under running water to wash away any sand or dirt.

Bring a large pot or a large deep skillet full of water to a boil over high heat. Add the leeks, reduce the heat a bit, cover the pot, and cook for 10 to 15 minutes, or until the leeks are very tender. Drain and rinse under cold water. Pat dry and gently press out any excess water.

Place the garlic in a small bowl. Whisk in the oil, mustard, vinegar, and fine sea salt to combine. Stir in the shallot.

When ready to serve, gently turn the leeks in the vinaigrette to coat them thoroughly, then arrange 2 leeks on each plate and drizzle some of the remaining vinaigrette over them. Sprinkle the walnuts and capers (if using) on top.

Baked Omelet Parmentier

SERVES 4

Anything cooked "parmentier" is made with potatoes. This substantial omelet with potatoes is a great lunch dish served with baguette slices, a glass of red wine, and a bit of arugula salad. It is also a forgiving recipe—one to which you can also add other ingredients, like caramelized onions, mushrooms, or grated cheese, if you wish.

FOR THE OMELET

Unsalted butter, for the pan

3 tablespoons extra-virgin olive oil

3 Yukon gold potatoes, peeled and cut into small dice

1/2 teaspoon fine sea salt, divided

1 garlic clove, pressed or minced

2 scallions, thinly sliced

7 large eggs, at room temperature

1 teaspoon Dijon mustard

1/4 teaspoon baking powder

Freshly ground black pepper

1/8 teaspoon ground nutmeg

1/2 cup minced fresh flat-leaf parsley leaves

1/2 cup minced fresh dill fronds

FOR THE SALAD

2 tablespoons extra-virgin olive oil

2 tablespoons freshly squeezed lemon juice

1 teaspoon Dijon mustard

1/8 teaspoon fine sea salt

4 cups arugula leaves

French baguette slices, for serving

TO MAKE THE OMELET: Preheat the oven to 375 degrees F. Coat the sides and bottom of an 8-inch cake pan generously with butter.

In a large skillet over medium heat, heat the oil. Toss in the potatoes and 1/4 teaspoon of fine sea salt, cover the skillet, and cook for 5 minutes, stirring once or twice. Add the garlic, stir to coat the potatoes, cover the pan, and cook for 5 minutes, or until the potatoes are tender and cooked through. Transfer them to the prepared cake pan. Scatter the scallions over the potatoes.

In a large bowl, whisk the eggs with the mustard, baking powder, remaining 1/4 teaspoon of fine sea salt, pepper to taste, and nutmeg to blend. Toss in the parsley and dill and whisk to combine. Pour the egg mixture over the vegetables in the cake pan.

Bake for about 8 minutes, just until the center is done and no longer runny. Do not overcook.

TO MAKE THE SALAD: While the omelet bakes, in a medium bowl, whisk the oil, lemon juice, mustard, and fine sea salt to blend. Add the arugula and toss to coat.

TO SERVE: Slice the omelet into wedges and place on plates. Place some arugula salad on the side and serve with the baguette slices.

Skillet Ratatouille with Eggs and Sourdough Toast

SERVES 4

Inspired by shakshuka, the Middle Eastern egg dish cooked in simmering vegetables and tomato sauce, I thought doing the same with a French ratatouille made sense. This French Provençal stewed vegetable dish that we all know and love turns out to be a great match for eggs.

For a twist on texture and to save time, instead of chopping all the vegetables by hand, I quickly put them through the shredding disk of a food processor.

1 medium zucchini, cut into thick pieces

1 small red bell pepper, cut into thick pieces

1 small eggplant, cut into thick pieces

1 medium onion, quartered

2 garlic cloves, halved

3 tablespoons extra-virgin olive oil

3 tablespoons tomato paste

¼ teaspoon fine sea salt

¼ cup water, plus more as needed

4 tomatoes, unpeeled, 3 left whole and 1 diced

½ cup fresh basil leaves, coarsely chopped

4 large eggs, at room temperature, or 8 large eggs (to serve 2 eggs per person)

4 tablespoons grated Parmesan, Gruyère, or Emmental cheese

1 cup minced fresh parsley leaves

8 thick slices sourdough bread, toasted and buttered

Using a food processor fitted with the shredding disk, one at a time, shred the zucchini, bell pepper, eggplant, onion, and garlic and toss each into a large bowl.

In a large skillet or cast-iron skillet over medium heat, stir together the oil, tomato paste, and fine sea salt and cook for 30 seconds. Add the shredded vegetables and water and stir to coat. Cover the skillet and cook for about 4 minutes until the vegetables are tender. Timing will vary depending on the size of the vegetable pieces.

Using the large holes of a box grater, grate the 3 whole tomatoes over the skillet. Stir in the basil and diced tomato. If the mixture is too thick, add a little water until it becomes spoonable. Stir well.

Turn the heat to medium-low. Crack the eggs onto the ratatouille, re-cover the skillet, and cook until the eggs are done to your liking.

Serve immediately, either in the skillet at the table or plated individually, sprinkled with grated cheese and parsley, with the toast to the side.

Spring Vegetable Ragoût with Preserved Lemon Sauce

Serve this ragoût on its own with crusty bread, or over pasta with a final flourish of grated Parmesan, if you like. You can use store-bought preserved lemons for this, or make your own. Preserved lemons, one of my most treasured refrigerator staples, are easy to make, taking only about 15 minutes to prepare, but then you wait 4 weeks before using them as they take that long to soften. It is worth it. Once you taste them in a salad dressing you will never look back. You can add their zing to braises and even to sweet lemon desserts. If you make your own preserved lemons, you will need a Mason jar with a lid (its size will determine how many lemons to buy). They can be kept refrigerated for up to 4 months, but mine never last that long and I make new batches continuously so I always have some on hand.

FOR THE PRESERVED LEMONS (OPTIONAL)

¾ cup sea salt, divided, plus more as needed

2 bay leaves

4 to 8 organic lemons, scrubbed and dried

FOR THE LEMON SAUCE

1 whole preserved lemon (per the recipe, or store-bought), rinsed and seeded

1 garlic clove, sliced

¼ cup extra-virgin olive oil

3 tablespoons water, plus more as needed

2 to 3 tablespoons honey, plus more as needed

2 tablespoons freshly squeezed lemon juice

1 teaspoon Dijon mustard

Sea salt (optional)

TO MAKE THE PRESERVED LEMONS: Wash and dry a Mason jar big enough to hold the amount of lemons you have and the lid well. Put 2 table-spoons of sea salt in the bottom of the jar, then toss in the bay leaves.

Slice off a bit of the ends of each lemon. Then, cutting vertically, about three-fourths of the way through the lemons, but not all the way as you want them attached at the bottom, quarter the lemons. Put a lemon in a small bowl and gently pull apart the quarters like flower petals. Pour sea salt into the lemons' cavities, about halfway up the lemon. Pack the lemons into the jar, pushing them down tightly onto one another. As you layer in the lemons, sprinkle in more sea salt to fill the crevices. When the jar is full, pour any sea salt left from the bowl over the top.

Use a wooden spoon to push the lemons down even more so they release some of their juice. At this point you might have room to add another lemon. Then, add another tablespoon of sea salt over the top. Screw on the lid. Leave the jar on the counter, out of direct sunlight, for 4 weeks, then begin to use the lemons. Keep refrigerated for up to 4 months.

TO MAKE THE LEMON SAUCE: In the bowl of a food processor, combine the preserved lemon, garlic, oil, water, honey, lemon juice, and mustard and process until smooth. Taste and adjust the sweetness or saltiness to your liking. Add water if you would like a thinner sauce. Set aside.

continued >>

FOR THE VEGETABLE RAGOÛT

2 cups chicken stock

1 pound green beans, trimmed and cut into 1-inch pieces

16 pitted green olives

8 very small new potatoes or fingerlings, halved

8 asparagus spears, woody ends trimmed, cut into 1-inch pieces

4 thin carrots, cut into 1-inch pieces

4 to 8 radishes, trimmed and halved

$\frac{1}{2}$ small head cauliflower, florets only, cut into small pieces

FOR THE GARNISHES

1 avocado, peeled, halved, pitted, and cut into small dice

1 red endive, thinly sliced

4 scallions, thinly sliced

$\frac{1}{4}$ cup fresh chives, minced

$\frac{1}{2}$ cup fresh flat-leaf parsley leaves, minced

French baguette slices, for serving

TO MAKE THE VEGETABLE RAGOÛT: Pour the chicken stock into a wide saucepan or skillet and bring to a boil over high heat, then reduce the heat to maintain a simmer and add the green beans, olives, potatoes, asparagus, carrots, radishes, and cauliflower. Cover the pan and simmer until all the vegetables are tender. Drain the vegetables into a colander.

TO GARNISH AND SERVE: Warm the lemon sauce on the stove while you divide the vegetables among four plates or shallow bowls. To each plate, add some avocado, endive, and scallions. Pour the warmed sauce over the top and sprinkle with the minced parsley. Serve the baguette slices to the side.

Green Pasta Pistou

The French adore their pasta! This beautiful dish is fresh and light and sings with herby goodness. It is made with pistou, a Provençal sauce similar to pesto but made without pine nuts.

FOR THE PISTOU

5 garlic cloves, peeled

6 ounces Parmesan cheese, sliced

2 cups tightly packed fresh basil leaves

1 teaspoon fine sea salt

1 cup extra-virgin olive oil

FOR THE PASTA

2 tablespoons fine sea salt

1 bunch kale leaves, stemmed and ribs removed

1 pound fettuccine or tagliatelle pasta

2 tablespoons extra-virgin olive oil

½ cup freshly grated Parmesan or Pecorino Romano cheese

TO MAKE THE PISTOU: In the bowl of a food processor, combine the garlic, Parmesan, basil, and fine sea salt and process for 5 seconds. With the machine running, slowly pour in the oil in a thin stream until well blended. Set aside.

TO MAKE THE PASTA: Bring a large pot full of water to a boil over high heat. Add the sea salt and toss in the kale leaves. Cook for 4 minutes. Using tongs or a slotted spoon, transfer the kale to a colander and run it under cold water to stop the cooking. Squeeze the kale dry, transfer to a cutting board, and chop coarsely. Set aside.

Return the water in the pot to a boil. Add the pasta and cook according to the package instructions. Reserve ¼ cup of the cooking water, then drain the pasta.

In a large skillet over medium heat, heat the oil. Add the pasta and reserved cooking water. Cook, stirring, for 1 minute. Add the pistou and kale and stir to blend. Remove from the heat, sprinkle the Parmesan over the pasta, cover for 1 minute, then serve.

Fluffy Cauliflower and Cheese Quiche

SERVES 6

To elevate a quiche to a lighter texture, beat the eggs for several minutes, which gives it a silky, almost fluffy consistency that works well with the cauliflower and cheese in this recipe. The other element that adds an intriguing undertone to the flavor is the Maldon smoked sea salt.

All-purpose flour to dust work surface

1 best quality store-bought piecrust, chilled for 1 hour

1 large egg white beaten with 1 teaspoon water

1 ½ cups large cauliflower florets

1 ¼ cups grated Gruyère or Emmental cheese

4 large eggs, at room temperature

1 cup half-and-half, at room temperature

2 teaspoons sugar

1 ½ teaspoons Maldon smoked sea salt flakes

⅛ teaspoon ground nutmeg

2 tablespoons snipped fresh chives

Roll out the chilled dough on a floured work surface to fit into a 9- or 10-inch pie pan, fluted tart pan, or tart pan with removable base, leaving a 1-inch overhang all around to allow for shrinkage. Crimp the edges of the dough to make a decorative rim for the crust. Pop the crust in the freezer while you preheat the oven.

Preheat the oven to 350 degrees F.

Line the crust with parchment paper and fill it halfway with rice or dried beans. Bake for 10 minutes. Remove the parchment with the rice or beans. Brush the crust with the egg wash and bake for 8 minutes. The egg wash will create a barrier so the crust does not become soggy. Remove from the oven.

Meanwhile, place the cauliflower florets in a large pot, add enough water to cover, and bring to a boil over high heat. Reduce the heat to medium-low and simmer until very tender. Drain and gently pat dry with paper towels or a clean kitchen towel. When cool to the touch, chop the cauliflower into smaller pieces and arrange in the crust.

Spread the grated cheese evenly over the cauliflower.

In a large bowl, using a handheld electric mixer, beat the eggs on high speed for 3 minutes. Add the half-and-half, sugar, smoked sea salt, and nutmeg and beat on high speed for 4 minutes, then pour the egg mixture over the ingredients in the pan. Place the pan on a baking sheet and into the oven. Bake for 45 minutes, or until the center is just set with slight jiggle. Let cool for 20 minutes, then serve with a sprinkle of chives.

Sweet Potatoes Dauphinoise

In the mountainous Savoy region of France, hearty dishes like this one are perfect after a day of skiing. Dauphinoise *is a dish of white potatoes baked in milk or cream. This version matches the sweetness of sweet potatoes with a salty Mornay sauce enriched with lots of cheese.*

4 tablespoons (½ stick) unsalted butter, plus more for the baking dish

4 cups thinly sliced peeled sweet potatoes

¼ cup all-purpose flour

2 ½ cups whole milk or half-and-half

3 garlic cloves, pressed or minced

2 tablespoons honey

2 teaspoons Dijon mustard

1 teaspoon freshly grated nutmeg

2 teaspoons fresh thyme leaves

1 teaspoon fine sea salt

1 ½ cups grated Gruyère, Raclette, or Emmental cheese

½ cup grated Parmesan cheese

Preheat the oven to 350 degrees F. Coat an 8 × 10-inch baking dish generously with butter.

Bring a large pot full of water to a boil over high heat, gently drop in the sweet potato slices, and boil for 6 minutes.

In a saucepan over medium heat, melt the butter. Whisk in the flour until coated and cook for 2 minutes, whisking constantly. Pour in the milk and, while whisking, cook for about 4 minutes, or until the sauce thickens. Stir in the garlic, honey, mustard, nutmeg, thyme, and fine sea salt to combine. Add the Gruyère and stir until it melts. You have just made a Mornay sauce, the same one you would make for mac and cheese.

Layer one-third of the sweet potatoes in the bottom of the prepared baking dish and pour one-third of the sauce over the sweet potatoes. Arrange another third of the sweet potatoes in a layer over the sauce and pour another one-third of the sauce on top. Create a final layer of sweet potatoes, covering them with the remaining sauce. Sprinkle the Parmesan over the top.

Cover the baking dish with a lid or aluminum foil and bake for 45 minutes to 1 hour 30 minutes, until the sweet potatoes are tender, depending on the thickness of the sweet potatoes. During the last 15 minutes or so, remove the cover while baking so the casserole browns a bit. Let rest for 15 minutes before serving.

Buttery Savoy Cabbage and Apple Chiffonade

SERVES 4

Savoy cabbage has been a veritable player in French cuisine since the mid-1500s. It is the green cabbage with the wrinkled outer leaves, tender inner leaves, and a slightly nutty flavor.

My favorite way to cook savoy cabbage is super simple, in the manner of an embeurrée de chou, *which is cabbage chiffonade, or sliced very thinly, then cooked in butter. Some people add diced potatoes, bacon, lentils, or onion.*

¼ teaspoon baking soda

1 small or ½ medium head savoy cabbage

2 sweet apples

5 tablespoons salted butter

Freshly ground black pepper

¼ teaspoon ground nutmeg

Sea salt (optional)

Bring a large pot full of water to a boil over high heat, then add the baking soda, which will keep the cabbage leaves green.

Trim the cabbage of its tougher outer leaves and discard. Cut out the core and slice the leaves into thin strips, or chiffonade. Toss into the boiling water and boil for 4 minutes, then drain in a colander.

While the cabbage cooks, peel the apples, cut them into slices, then cut them again into thin strips about the same thickness of the cabbage slices.

In a Dutch oven or deep wide skillet over medium heat, melt the butter. Toss in the apples, cabbage, pepper to taste, and nutmeg and stir to coat. Sauté for 4 minutes, or until the apples and cabbage are as tender as you like them. Check for seasoning and add sea salt, if desired. Serve hot.

Broccoli and Carrot Purée

This is a staple on my buffet or holiday table, presented in one large bowl with the broccoli purée filling half the bowl and the carrot purée filling the other half, so they are side by side. Both are light and smooth and flavorful.

FOR THE BROCCOLI PURÉE

6 cups green or purple broccoli florets

4 tablespoons (½ stick) unsalted butter, cubed

1 teaspoon sea salt flakes

⅛ teaspoon ground nutmeg

FOR THE CARROT PURÉE

6 cups sliced carrots

4 tablespoons (½ stick) unsalted butter, cubed

1 teaspoon sea salt flakes

¼ cup ginger jam, or apricot or orange marmalade

⅛ teaspoon ground nutmeg

TO MAKE THE BROCCOLI PURÉE: Place the broccoli in a large pot, add enough water to cover, and bring to a boil over high heat. Reduce the heat to medium and cook until very tender. Drain the broccoli and transfer to the bowl of a food processor and, while still hot, add the butter, sea salt flakes, and nutmeg. Pulse 12 times, or until smooth. Transfer to a bowl and keep warm. Clean the food processor.

TO MAKE THE CARROT PURÉE: Place the carrots in a large pot, add enough water to cover, and bring to a boil over high heat. Reduce the heat to medium and cook until very tender. Drain the carrots and transfer to the bowl of a food processor and, while still hot, add the butter, sea salt flakes, jam, and nutmeg to the food processor with the cooked carrots and purée until smooth

When ready to serve, scoop the broccoli into one half of a serving bowl and the carrot purée into the other half.

DESSERTS

I wrote a whole book called *French Desserts*, so you just know I love them!

In fact, I can't go anywhere in France without popping into a pastry shop, *pâtisserie*, to at least look if not sample. My sweet addiction extends from a chocolate or almond croissant in the morning to dessert after lunch to driving miles if I hear about a shop or restaurant making an amazing sweet for dessert after dinner. And, don't get me started on chocolates! I think French chocolates are the best.

The French buy their sweets, like I do, at pâtisseries, and their chocolates from the maestros that abound there, but at home they opt for making less elaborate fare. They might make a simple sweet loaf cake, a fruit salad, poach some stone fruit, or make a chocolate mousse or flan. The following recipes will take you into a French home so you can taste their beloved desserts.

Easy Fresh Apricot Jam
on a Cheese Board

SERVES AS MANY AS DESIRED

Charles de Gaulle once famously said, "How can anyone govern a nation that has 246 different kinds of cheese?" And I famously replied, "How can anyone try all 246 different kinds of cheese?" Not that I haven't tried. Everywhere I go, I search out the local cheeses and relish learning about them. That is to explain why I nearly always serve some form of cheese board after dinner, because I love my cheese! What I choose depends mostly upon what I find in the markets that day, but here are my favorites that usually end up on my cheese board. They should all be served at room temperature.

Butter: *Good French butter with flakes of salt mixed in; if I can't find one, I buy good unsalted French butter and serve it with flakes of salt sprinkled on top.*

Camembert: *From the happy bovines in Camembert, Normandy, who are responsible for this lovely relatively mild cheese; press on the middle to make sure it is soft and not firm.*

Cantal: *A firm cheese great for slicing and fanning on your board.*

Goat cheese: *There are so many goat cheeses made in France and they all are so different in flavor but a couple that seem to be available everywhere are Bucheron and Crottin de Chavignol, both from the Loire Valley.*

Roquefort: *A fabulous strong blue cheese from the village of Roquefort-sur-Soulzon; place this at the end of the cheese board to be eaten last. A bleu d'Auvergne from the Rhône-Alpes region is much milder and quite creamy and a budget-friendly alternative.*

Serve the cheeses with this quick homemade apricot jam. When you present the jam on the cheese board, surround it with the French cheeses you have chosen and some walnuts. Slices of store-bought smoked duck arranged in small piles would also be a nice addition. Arrange crackers and baguette slices nearby.

You can make this jam in under an hour of active time. Keep it refrigerated until use. Make it the day before you need it so it has time to work its magic overnight in your refrigerator.

2 pounds fresh apricots, unpeeled, halved, and pitted

3 cups sugar

Grated zest of ½ organic lemon or orange

3 tablespoons freshly squeezed lemon juice

½ teaspoon ground cardamom

¼ cup water or white wine

½ teaspoon vanilla extract

Slice the apricots into a large bowl. Add the sugar, lemon zest, lemon juice, and cardamom and stir to combine. Cover the bowl and refrigerate overnight to macerate. This should produce some liquid that will make a lovely jam.

When you are ready to make the jam, pour the apricot mixture into a heavy-bottomed pot or Dutch oven, add the water and vanilla, and bring to a boil over high heat. Reduce the heat to maintain a low boil and cook for about 20 minutes, stirring frequently, until the jam thickens. Skim off and discard any foam. Remove from the heat and let cool. Serve immediately, or ladle into Mason jars with lids and keep refrigerated for up to 7 days.

Roasted Pears with
Honey Ice Cream and Sea Salt

French honey is fantastic. I opt for French honey in so many recipes, even savory, because of its depth of flavor and the sheer variety you can find. This honey ice cream brings big flavor to the roasted pears, which intensifies their sweetness.

Make the ice cream a day ahead, as most ice cream machines require you to put the elements in the freezer to chill, and the ice cream takes time to freeze. Also, use local honey if you can, or buckwheat honey. Local honey has much more flavor than those found in the supermarket. Your homemade honey ice cream will be like a scoop of heaven.

FOR THE HONEY ICE CREAM

5 large egg yolks, at room temperature

1 cup whole milk

2 cups heavy cream

Neutral oil, for the measuring cup

$\frac{1}{2}$ cup honey

1 teaspoon ground cinnamon

1 teaspoon almond extract

$\frac{1}{2}$ teaspoon vanilla extract

FOR THE PEARS

4 firm pears, unpeeled, halved, and cored

3 tablespoons water

$\frac{1}{2}$ teaspoon ground cinnamon

$\frac{1}{4}$ cup honey, warmed until liquid

Sea salt flakes

TO MAKE THE HONEY ICE CREAM: In a mixing bowl and using a hand-held electric mixer, beat the egg yolks until they are pale yellow and thick.

In a saucepan over medium heat, heat the milk and heavy cream until little bubbles form around the edge of the saucepan. Remove from the heat. Slowly whisk $\frac{1}{2}$ cup of the hot milk and cream mixture into the beaten eggs to temper the eggs (so the hot mixture does not scramble them). While whisking, pour the tempered egg mixture into the saucepan, put the saucepan on medium-low heat, and slowly cook, whisking, until it slightly thickens and is a custard consistency that coats the back of a spoon. An instant-read thermometer should register 165 to 170 degrees F.

Fill a large bowl with ice water.

Coat a measuring cup lightly with oil before adding the honey so it slips out easily into the saucepan. Add the honey, cinnamon, almond extract, and vanilla and quickly whisk to combine. Pour the custard mixture into a bowl and place the bowl in the ice bath for about 10 minutes to cool.

Cover the bowl of custard, refrigerate for 5 hours, then process in your ice cream machine according to the manufacturer's instructions. Transfer the ice cream to a covered container and freeze for 5 hours, or overnight, before using.

continued >>

TO MAKE THE PEARS: An hour or two before you plan to serve the dessert, roast the pears.

Preheat the oven to 350 degrees F.

Arrange the pears, cut-side up, in a baking dish and pour the water around them. Sprinkle the pears with the cinnamon. Cover the baking dish with aluminum foil and bake for 25 to 30 minutes, or until tender. Keep warm until ready to serve.

When ready, remove the ice cream from the freezer. If it is too hard, let sit at room temperature for 10 minutes before scooping.

Place the warm pears on serving plates and put a scoop of ice cream in the well of each. Drizzle each with a little warm honey and top with a sprinkle of sea salt flakes.

Caramelized Plums with Sweet Goat Cheese Mousse

Yellow, green, purple, red, bluish-purple, you can use any color plums for this recipe, or a combination. This recipe produces a jammy texture that melts in your mouth and is delicious with the sweet cloud of goat cheese you serve it with.

Grab a bag of plums when you are at the market. You'll want to buy more than you need for this recipe as they make a juicy snack on the way home and are great baked with a roast, incorporated into a tagine, or added to a stuffing for chicken.

FOR THE GOAT CHEESE MOUSSE

½ cup heavy cream, chilled

1 tablespoon powdered sugar, plus more as needed

7 ounces soft goat cheese, at room temperature

½ cup whole milk

FOR THE PLUMS

2 tablespoons unsalted butter

2 tablespoons light brown sugar

¼ teaspoon fine sea salt

8 ripe plums, halved and pitted

Balsamic vinegar to garnish

TO MAKE THE GOAT CHEESE MOUSSE: In a medium bowl and using an electric handheld mixer, whip the heavy cream on high speed until stiff peaks form. Whip in the powdered sugar.

In another medium bowl and using a handheld electric mixer with clean beaters, whip the goat cheese on high speed until softened. Add the milk and beat until smooth. Spoon in one-third of the whipped cream and fold to blend. Gently fold in the remaining whipped cream until just mixed. Taste and whisk in more powdered sugar, as needed. Cover and refrigerate the goat cheese mousse until ready to use.

TO MAKE THE PLUMS: In a skillet large enough to hold all the plum halves over medium-low heat, melt the butter. Add the brown sugar and fine sea salt and cook for 2 minutes. Arrange the plums in the skillet, flesh-side down, cover the pan, and cook for 10 minutes, or a bit longer, until they are soft but still in shape.

Divide the plums among four plates. Drizzle with a little vinegar, then spoon on dollops of the whipped goat cheese mousse to serve.

Homemade Crème Fraîche and Raspberry Parfaits

SERVES 4

Making homemade crème fraîche is easy, requiring only two ingredients: buttermilk and heavy cream. Just make sure you buy cultured buttermilk and pasteurized heavy cream (not ultra-pasteurized). You make it a couple of days ahead and all of a sudden you have the most luxurious homemade crème fraîche, ready to make this parfait, which you present in simple glasses or martini glasses.

FOR THE CRÈME FRAÎCHE

2 cups pasteurized heavy (whipping) cream

6 tablespoons buttermilk with live cultures

7 tablespoons sugar

½ teaspoon vanilla extract

FOR THE PARFAITS

2 cups fresh raspberries

4 fresh mint leaves

TO MAKE THE CRÈME FRAÎCHE: Make the crème fraîche 2 days ahead. Pour the heavy cream and buttermilk into a clean quart-size Mason jar or bowl and cover with cheesecloth or a clean kitchen towel secured with twine. Let sit on the counter at room temperature for 2 days to thicken.

Whisk in the sugar and vanilla. Seal the lid on the jar, or cover with plastic wrap if in a bowl, and refrigerate until ready to use.

TO MAKE THE PARFAITS: Place ¼ cup of berries into the bottom of each glass. Dollop two-thirds of the crème fraîche over the berries, dividing it evenly among the glasses. Arrange the rest of the berries over the crème fraîche, then divide the remaining crème fraîche over the top. Garnish each glass with a mint leaf.

Red Wine–Poached Cherries and Grapes with Cardamom Chantilly

SERVES 4

This is a vin chaud *poaching liquid made with red wine, sugar, spices, and orange peel that you cook fresh cherries and grapes in, then top with a cloud of sweet cardamom whipped cream. A sugar cookie to the side would be a nice addition.*

2 ½ cups dry red wine

1 small organic orange

½ cup granulated sugar

½ cup packed light brown sugar

2 cinnamon sticks

4 whole cloves

1 teaspoon vanilla extract

1 ½ pounds fresh cherries, halved and pitted

8 ounces seedless grapes, halved

1 cup heavy (whipping) cream, chilled

2 tablespoons powdered sugar

1 teaspoon ground cardamom

⅛ teaspoon freshly grated nutmeg

Coarse sea salt flakes

Pour the wine into a saucepan. Slice off a big strip of orange peel and toss it into the wine, saving the orange for another purpose. Add the granulated and brown sugars, cinnamon sticks, cloves, and vanilla. Bring to a simmer over medium heat, stirring until the sugar melts. Turn the heat to low and cook for 10 minutes to infuse the wine with the spices.

Add the cherries and grapes, return the liquid to a simmer, cover the pan, and cook for about 6 minutes until the cherries are just tender. Transfer the fruit and the liquid to a large bowl, removing and discarding the cinnamon stick, orange peel, and cloves, and let cool.

When ready to serve, in a medium bowl, combine the heavy cream, powdered sugar, cardamom, and nutmeg. Using a handheld electric mixer, whip the cream on high speed until stiff peaks form.

Divide the fruit and poaching liquid among four bowls and top each with a dollop of cardamom whipped cream, then a small sprinkle of coarse sea salt flakes.

Floating Islands on Fresh Strawberry Sauce

SERVES 4

I make oeufs à la neige, *or floating islands, in a microwave and it works so well that I want to share the process with you for this stunning meringue dessert floating on fresh raw strawberry sauce. Serve in cocktail glasses or shallow bowls.*

FOR THE STRAWBERRY SAUCE

2 pounds fresh strawberries, stemmed and hulled

6 tablespoons powdered sugar, plus more as needed

2 tablespoons Cointreau or Grand Marnier

1 tablespoon honey, plus more as needed

1 teaspoon vanilla extract

FOR THE FLOATING ISLANDS

8 large egg whites, at room temperature

$\frac{1}{4}$ teaspoon cream of tartar

$\frac{1}{8}$ teaspoon fine sea salt

$\frac{1}{2}$ cup granulated sugar

8 fresh strawberries, sliced

TO MAKE THE STRAWBERRY SAUCE: In the bowl of a food processor or a blender, combine the strawberries, powdered sugar, Cointreau, honey, and vanilla and process until smooth. Taste and add more honey or sugar if your strawberries are not sweet enough, and a bit of water, if desired, to make the sauce more pourable. Cover and refrigerate until ready to use.

TO MAKE THE FLOATING ISLANDS: In a large bowl, combine the egg whites, cream of tartar, and fine sea salt. Using a handheld electric mixer, beat the whites on high speed until they form soft peaks. Continue beating while pouring in the granulated sugar until the peaks are stiff and shiny. Form the whites into 4 "egg" shapes. Place one on a microwave-safe plate and microwave on high power for 10 seconds. Repeat with the remaining meringues.

To serve, divide the strawberry sauce among four shallow bowls, float 1 "egg" on the sauce in each bowl, and arrange the sliced strawberries around the eggs.

Pont Neuf Baked Figs with Brie, Walnuts, and Honey

SERVES 4

Years ago, there was a bistro that was a short walk from the Pont Neuf that made this dessert. It's not there anymore but the memory of their dessert made with fresh figs lives on as I attempt to recreate its taste and texture at home. The figs are warm and sweet, the Brie melted, and the honey, thyme, and walnuts take it over the top.

Unsalted butter, for the muffin tin

8 fat fresh figs, rinsed and dried

1 (8-ounce) wheel Brie cheese

2 teaspoons fresh thyme leaves

8 walnut halves

8 tablespoons honey

8 French baguette slices

Preheat the oven to 350 degrees F. Coat an 8-cup muffin tin generously with butter. If you prefer, you can bake the figs on a baking sheet or in a baking dish.

With a small sharp knife, cut a cross (make two intersecting slices) into the top of each fig. Put the figs into the muffin tin so they sit up straight, with the cross at the top. Gently pull open each cross so there is a cavity to tuck the cheese into.

Slice the Brie into 8 pieces, then insert 1 piece into the cavity of each fig. Sprinkle the thyme over the cheese. Put one walnut half on top of each fig, then drizzle each with 1 tablespoon of honey.

Bake for 8 to 10 minutes until the cheese is melted. Serve 2 on each plate with baguette slices.

Last-Minute
Grand Marnier Crêpes Suzette

SERVES 4

My father used to amaze us making crêpes when we were children. He would ceremoniously present the copper chafing dish and its burner that he bought at E. Dehillerin in Paris onto our dining room table. He would flambé the crêpes theatrically with Grand Marnier after he cooked them, spoon the delectable sauce slowly over the crêpes, then plate them and make us wait until he scooped his homemade vanilla ice cream over the top. Oh, what a treat.

I do the same for company or on holidays, but when I am hit with nostalgia yet don't have time I resort to a few shortcuts. Instead of making the crêpes, I will use store-bought ones that they usually sell near the fruit in grocery stores, fresh orange juice, and top with top-quality store-bought ice cream. These, then, are my last-minute crêpes Suzette.

8 store-bought French dessert crêpes

1 (12-ounce) jar thick-cut orange marmalade

6 tablespoons (¾ stick) unsalted butter

4 organic oranges, scrubbed and dried, 2 left unpeeled and whole, 2 oranges peeled and sectioned

3 tablespoons granulated sugar, plus more as needed

2 tablespoons Grand Marnier, plus more as needed

Powdered sugar, to garnish

4 scoops vanilla ice cream

Preheat the oven to 150 degrees F. Line a baking sheet with parchment paper.

Place the crêpes on the prepared baking sheet and spread each with 1 ½ tablespoons of marmalade, all the way to the edges. Fold in half, then fold in half again to make a triangle. Cover the crêpes with aluminum foil and place in the oven to warm.

Meanwhile, in a skillet over medium heat, melt the butter. Grate the zest of 1 whole orange into the butter, then juice that orange and the other whole orange into the pan. Whisk in the granulated sugar.

Off the heat, pour in the Grand Marnier. Put the skillet back on the stove and, over high heat, bring to a boil and boil for 1 ½ minutes. Taste and add more granulated sugar or Grand Marnier, if desired. Add the orange sections and cook until they are warm.

Place two warm, filled crêpes on each dessert plate. Ladle the sauce over the top, sprinkle with powdered sugar through a fine-mesh sieve, and serve with a scoop of vanilla ice cream.

Clafoutis with Loads of Berries

SERVES 8

Traditional French clafoutis is made with whole cherries, but you can use any fruit depending on the season. If I happen to have an orange, I will zest it and add some to the batter as well. The secret to making a tender clafoutis is to let the batter rest for at least 30 minutes before pouring it in the baking dish. In the end, you will be rewarded with a celestial cloud of berry goodness.

Unsalted butter, for the baking dish

1 cup fresh raspberries

1 cup fresh blueberries

1 ¼ cups whole milk, at room temperature

¾ cup granulated sugar, divided

3 large eggs, at room temperature

1 ½ teaspoons vanilla extract

1 ½ teaspoons almond extract

¼ teaspoon fine sea salt

½ cup all-purpose flour

Grated zest of 1 organic orange (optional)

Powdered sugar, to garnish

Coat a 10-inch baking dish generously with butter, then scatter the raspberries and blueberries on the bottom of the dish.

In a blender, combine the milk, ½ cup of granulated sugar, the eggs, vanilla, almond extract, fine sea salt, flour, and orange zest (if using). Blend well for about 15 seconds, then let the batter rest for 30 minutes.

After 15 minutes, preheat the oven to 400 degrees F.

Pour the rested batter over the berries and sprinkle the remaining ¼ cup of granulated sugar over the top.

Bake for about 45 minutes until the top is puffed and browned and a toothpick into the center comes out clean.

Before serving, using a fine-mesh sieve, sprinkle some powdered sugar over the top.

Savoie Cake Drenched with Peach Melba

SERVES 6

A recipe dating back to the fourteenth century, this ancient cake is popular in the Haute-Savoie region in the French Alps. Although the cake is light and fluffy, it is amazingly sturdy and super easy to make. I serve it with fresh peaches and raspberries, with a good soaking of their juices.

FOR THE CAKE

Unsalted butter, for the soufflé dish

Granulated sugar, for the soufflé dish

⅓ cup all-purpose flour

½ cup cornstarch

1 teaspoon baking powder

4 large eggs, at room temperature, separated

½ cup powdered sugar, plus more to garnish

½ teaspoon ground cinnamon

1 teaspoon vanilla extract

½ teaspoon almond extract

Pinch fine sea salt

FOR THE PEACH MELBA

4 cups fresh raspberries

2 tablespoons water or Grand Marnier, plus more as needed

2 tablespoons superfine sugar or powdered sugar, plus more as needed

4 ripe peaches

Juice of ½ organic lemon

TO MAKE THE CAKE: Preheat the oven to 350 degrees F. Cut a circle of parchment paper to fit into the bottom of an 8-inch soufflé dish or springform pan. Coat the bottom and sides of the soufflé dish generously with butter, then fit the parchment paper into the bottom. Coat the parchment with butter, then coat the bottom and sides of the soufflé dish generously with granulated sugar.

Sift the flour, cornstarch, and baking powder into a large bowl.

In a medium bowl and using a handheld electric mixer, beat the egg yolks on high speed for about 2 minutes until fluffy and pale yellow. Sift the powdered sugar and cinnamon over the egg yolks and beat on high speed for 6 minutes. Add the vanilla and almond extract and beat to combine.

In a large bowl and using a handheld mixer with clean beaters, beat the egg whites with a pinch of fine sea salt on medium speed for 2 minutes. Increase the speed to medium-high and beat for 2 minutes, then beat on high speed for 2 minutes until stiff peaks form.

Very gently fold the flour mixture into the yolks. It will be thick.

Fold one-third of the beaten whites into the egg yolk mixture, then a bit more, then the remaining whites, very gently so as not to deflate the batter. Pour the batter into the prepared dish.

Bake for 30 minutes.

continued >>

TO MAKE THE PEACH MELBA: While the cake bakes, in a blender, combine the raspberries, water, and superfine sugar. Blend until smooth. Transfer to a bowl and reserve. If you prefer, pass the sauce through a fine-mesh sieve to remove the raspberry seeds. Taste and add sugar, as needed, or more water to make a pourable sauce.

Remove the cake from the oven and let cool for 5 minutes. If you used a soufflé dish, carefully run a knife around the edges of the cake. Place a plate on top of the soufflé dish, turn both upside-down, and unmold the cake onto the plate. If you used a springform pan, unlock and remove the rim.

TO FINISH AND SERVE: Peel and slice the peaches into a large bowl, then toss them with the lemon juice.

Place a slice of cake on each plate. Ladle a generous amount of the raspberry sauce over half of the cake slice, add some peaches, and sift a little powdered sugar over the top.

Quick and Easy Caramelized Apple and Camembert Tatin

SERVES 6

For tarte Tatin *purists, this is an equally delicious, much quicker method for making fall's coziest French dessert. I find variations of this recipe all over French cooking magazines. It might have originated in Normandy as many of those recipes spike the apples with Calvados and incorporate Camembert, which is also from Normandy. Serve it warm with a scoop of ice cream.*

When I serve this to company, I serve it with cups of espresso with a sugar cube spiked with Calvados at the bottom of each cup.

5 large Granny Smith apples, peeled and cored

¼ cup packed light brown sugar

¾ teaspoon ground cinnamon

2 tablespoons salted butter

1 tablespoon granulated sugar

½ teaspoon fine sea salt

1 (8-ounce) wheel Camembert cheese, rind removed, thinly sliced

1 sheet store-bought all-butter puff pastry, thawed according to the package instructions

All-purpose flour, for dusting

Preheat the oven to 350 degrees F.

Line the bottom of an 8- or 9-inch cake pan or pie plate with parchment paper.

Cut the apples into ½-inch slices. Place the slices in a large bowl and toss them with the brown sugar and cinnamon to coat. Set aside for 15 minutes, then drain any liquid that accumulates at the bottom of the bowl.

In a large skillet over medium heat, melt the butter, then turn the heat to high. Toss in all the sliced apples and stir to coat. Cook on high heat for about 3 minutes without moving the apples. Flip them, sprinkle with the granulated sugar, and cook for 2 to 3 minutes more to caramelize the apples. Watch carefully and don't let them burn, but allow them to brown. Transfer the apples to prepared cake pan and spread into an even layer with a spatula. Sprinkle on the fine sea salt. Distribute the Camembert pieces evenly over the apples.

Lightly dust a clean work surface with flour and place the puff pastry sheet on it. Roll out the sheet so it's large enough to fit the pan with a couple inches overhanging all around. Fit the pastry over the pan and tuck the edges into the pan, creating a thicker crust. With a sharp knife, make 4 small slits in the top.

Bake for 40 to 45 minutes or until the crust is golden on top. Remove and let rest for 1 minute. Put a serving plate over the top, flip both over quickly, and unmold the tarte Tatin.

Tart Lemon Loaf Cake with Blackberries, Raspberries, and Blueberries

SERVES 8

Anything sweet and very lemony and I am sold. This humble little lemon loaf packs an impressive amount of lemon flavor.

FOR THE LOAF CAKE

1 tablespoon melted unsalted butter, plus more for the pan

2 cups cake flour, plus more for the pan

1 ½ cups granulated sugar

1 organic lemon

2 ½ teaspoons baking powder

¼ teaspoon fine sea salt

¼ teaspoon ground cinnamon

2 large eggs, at room temperature

1 large egg yolk, at room temperature

1 cup plain Greek-style yogurt

⅔ cups freshly squeezed lemon juice, divided

¼ cup vegetable oil

½ teaspoon vanilla extract

TO MAKE THE LOAF CAKE: Preheat the oven to 350 degrees F. Coat a 5 × 9-inch loaf pan with butter and dust it with flour, knocking out the excess.

Place the granulated sugar into the bowl of a food processor. Using a box grater, zest the lemon over the sugar. Process for 10 seconds, let rest for 10 minutes so the lemon oil scents the sugar, then transfer to a small bowl.

In a medium bowl, sift together the flour, baking powder, fine sea salt, and cinnamon.

In the bowl of a food processor, combine the eggs, egg yolk, yogurt, ⅓ cup lemon juice, oil, melted butter, and vanilla and process for 5 seconds. Add the lemon sugar and the flour mixture and pulse only until just combined, about 4 long pulses. Transfer the batter into the prepared loaf pan.

Bake for 50 to 55 minutes until golden and a tester inserted into the center comes out clean. Remove and let cool for 10 minutes. Remove the loaf from the pan, then wrap the loaf completely with plastic wrap and let cool. Wrapping keeps it moist.

FOR THE FRUIT

1 cup fresh blackberries, divided

1 cup fresh raspberries, divided

1 cup fresh blueberries, divided

¼ cup granulated sugar

1 cup heavy (whipping) cream, cold

2 tablespoons powdered sugar, plus more as needed

⅔ cup vanilla Greek-style yogurt

TO MAKE THE FRUIT: In a medium bowl combine ¼ cup each of the blackberries, raspberries, and blueberries and the granulated sugar. Using a potato masher or fork, mash the berries, then toss in the remaining whole blackberries, raspberries, and blueberries, stir, and let sit to macerate for 20 minutes.

When you are ready to serve, in a medium bowl and using a handheld electric mixer, beat the heavy cream with the powdered sugar on high speed until stiff peaks form. Gently fold in the vanilla yogurt, then taste and add more powdered sugar, as needed.

Brush the cake lightly all over with remaining ⅓ cup of lemon juice. Slice the cake and put 1 slice on each plate. Spoon on some whipped cream and top with the mixed berries and any of their juices from the bowl.

Fruity Frosty Cantaloupe Sorbet

You can almost smell the melons when you drive through the village of Cavaillon in Provence, the melon capital of France. I am kidding, of course, but they are that sweet and fragrant when they ripen. When that happens, I make everything melon: cold soup, melon balls, salad, and this wonderful sorbet, served with a slice of the intensely sweet and juicy Cavaillon melon, named after the village.

1 medium ripe cantaloupe, seeded, peeled, and coarsely chopped, plus cantaloupe wedges, to garnish

½ cup sugar

2 tablespoons hot water

2 tablespoons rum

3 tablespoons freshly squeezed lemon or lime juice

Toss the chopped cantaloupe into the bowl of a food processor and process until very smooth.

In a small bowl, whisk the sugar and hot water until the sugar dissolves, then pour this into the food processor. Add the rum and lemon juice and process for 40 seconds. Transfer to a covered container and refrigerate for 3 hours.

Pour the cantaloupe mixture into your ice cream maker and process according to the manufacturer's instructions. Scoop into a covered freezer container and freeze for 4 hours.

Scoop the sorbet into serving bowls or martini glasses and serve with a wedge of fresh cantaloupe tucked into the side of the bowl or glass.

ACKNOWLEDGMENTS

As always, I want to express deep gratitude to my longtime agent and friend, Deborah Ritchken, whose deep love for France matches mine.

To my loyal recipe testers who have been advising and sending in critiques, I thank you from the bottom of my heart, especially Shawnie Kelley, Barbara Michelson, Gabi Marshall, Kathleen Mills Frizzell, Sarah Hodge, Leah Klein, Violet Trout, Gloria Kobrin, and Zuffar Haq.

To Michelle Branson, my wonderful editor at Gibbs Smith, you make the experience of creating something beautiful a reality for me and I am forever grateful for your wisdom and kindness.

As always, my sincere thanks go to the entire team at Gibbs Smith for their extreme professionalism, enthusiasm, and for designing such beautiful books.

INDEX

Metric Conversion Chart

VOLUME MEASUREMENTS		WEIGHT MEASUREMENTS		TEMPERATURE CONVERSION	
U.S.	Metric	U.S.	Metric	Fahrenheit	Celsius
1 teaspoon	5 ml	½ ounce	15 g	250	120
1 tablespoon	15 ml	1 ounce	30 g	300	150
¼ cup	60 ml	3 ounces	90 g	325	160
⅓ cup	75 ml	4 ounces	115 g	350	180
½ cup	125 ml	8 ounces	225 g	375	190
⅔ cup	150 ml	12 ounces	350 g	400	200
¾ cup	175 ml	1 pound	450 g	425	220
1 cup	250 ml	2¼ pounds	1 kg	450	230

ABOUT THE AUTHOR

Hillary Davis is a cookbook author, contributing journalist, cooking instructor, and lecturer.

After the critical success of her first book, *A Million A Minute*, a book agent who knew about Hillary's love of all things food approached her and convinced her that a book about the Michelin star chefs working in London at the time would be a project they should start working on producing.

Hillary concurred and spent the better part of a year working gratis in the kitchens of Michelin starred chefs in London, peeling mountains of potatoes and whisking mounds of hollandaise in return for being allowed to spend time with the chefs in their kitchens for research for her cookbook proposal. Although the book never came to fruition, the long hours spent learning, interviewing the front room and sommeliers, and interviewing the Michelin star chefs (Marco Pierre White, Gordon Ramsay, Nobu, Jean-Christophe Novelli, Bruno Loubet, Pierre Koffman, and others) served her well.

Later, from her home in the south of France, Hillary wrote her first cookbook, *Cuisine Niçoise*. Davis lived in France for over thirteen years, two in Paris and over eleven in the south of France in the hilltop village of Bar-sur-Loup on the French Riviera. *Cuisine Niçoise* celebrated the healthy style of cooking prepared in the countryside around her home near Nice. She learned to cook this relatively unknown cuisine from neighbors in her village, friends, chefs, and a host of characters she met and talks about in her book.

In *French Comfort Food* she went further afield on a delicious journey throughout the many regions of France to re-discover the most loved meals that French families prepare every day at home. She has written two more French cookbooks: *Le French Oven*, *French Desserts*, and a cookbook about the cuisine of the Hamptons called *The Hamptons Kitchen*. Hillary also writes a popular weekly Substack newsletter called *DestinationFood*.

Hillary has a degree in economics from Columbia University in New York and a graduate degree in international relations from Cambridge University in England. She currently lives in the Hamptons, New York City, and lives several months a year in France.